NURSING RESEARCH & STATISTICS BSC NURSING 3RD YEAR

CHAPTER WISE SOLVED QUESTIONS AND ANSWERS

RUTWIK UPENDRA BHALSHANKAR

Copyright © Rutwik Upendra Bhalshankar
All Rights Reserved.

Contents

CHAPTER ONE

Introduction To Nursing Research

Q1. Define Research
= The word research derives from the French recherché, from researcher, to search closely where chercher means to search. The word research means 'to search again' or 'to examine carefully'.
DEFINITIONS OF RESEARCH

1. Research is defined as the search for knowledge or any systematic investigation to establish facts.

Chrish Jordan.

1. Research means search for facts or ideas and to answer the questions in order to find a solution to the problem.

-Horton.

3. Research essentially is a problem solving process, a systematic, intensive study directed towards full scientific knowledge of subject studie -

Ruth M.French.

4.Research is a process of systematically search for new events and relationships -**Notter.**

Q2. CHARACTERISTICS OF RESEARCH

= Research is defined as the search for knowledge or any systematic investigation to establish facts.

Chrish Jordan.

Research means search for facts or ideas and to answer the questions in order to find a solution to the problem.

-Horton.

CHARACTERISTICS OF RESEARCH ARE AS FOLLOW

1. Research attempts to solve a problem.

2. Research should be clearly defined and common concept to be used. 3. Research should be logical.

4. Research involves gathering new data from primary or firsthand sources or using existing data for new purposes.

5. Research is based upon observable experience or empirical evidence. 6. Research demands accurate observation and description.

7. Research generally employs careful designed procedures and rigorous analysis.

8. Research requires courage.

9. Research should be replicated.

10. Research should systematic.

11. Research analysis should be sufficient.

12. Research procedure should be described in a sufficient way.

13. Research conclusions should be confined to justify the data of the research.

14. Research conclusions should be confined to justify the data of the research.

15. Research emphasis the development of generalizations, principles or theories that will help in understanding, perdition and control.

Q 3. PURPOSE OF RESEARCH

= Research is defined as the search for knowledge or any systematic investigation to establish facts.

Chrish Jordan.

Research means search for facts or ideas and to answer the questions in order to find a solution to the problem.

-Horton.

PURPOSE OF RESEARCH

1. It unravels the mysteries of life.

2. It aims to analyze interrelations between variables and to derive causal explanations.

3. It aids planning and helps in national development.

4. It aims at finding solutions to problems.

5. It helps in the development of general laws.

6. It aims at developing new tools, concepts and theories for better study of unknown phenomena

7. It extends knowledge of human being regarding social life and environment.

8. It verifies existing facts and theory and these in turn help in improving our knowledge and ability to handle situations and events.

Q 4. SCOPE OF RESEARCH

= Research is defined as the search for knowledge or any systematic investigation to establish facts.

Chrish Jordan.

Research means search for facts or ideas and to answer the questions in order to find a solution to the problem.

-Horton.

SCOPE OF RESEARCH

1. It promotes scientific and legal thinking.

2. Operational: it is involved in solving operational problems, e.g., industries, factories etc

3. It is also used as an aim to economic policy and has gained its importance in government and business.

4. It helps in planning budget for the nation.

5. It facilitates the decisions of poly maker.

6. It is concerned necessary with the allocation of nation resources.

7. It studies the economic and social structure of nation and gives a detailed account of the change taking place in society. Introduction to Research

8. It helps in predicting future development.

9. It studies the motivation underlying the consumer behavior.

10. It helps the social scientist in studying social relationship and seeking answers for various social problems

11. It helps in the attainment of high position in social structure.

12. It helps in development of new ideas and insight for analysis for generation of new theories.

13. It helps to identify new facts as an advancement of a profession.

14. It is a measure of means of attaining live hood for professionals.

Q 5. QUALITIES OF GOOD RESEARCHER

= Research is defined as the search for knowledge or any systematic investigation to establish facts.

Chrish Jordan.

Research means search for facts or ideas and to answer the questions in order to find a solution to the problem.

-Horton.

QUALITIES OF GOOD RESEARCHER

1. Method of approach: The researcher should adopt correct procedure for identifying a problem and then for working on it, to find a solution for that problem.

2. Knowledge: The researcher should be well aware and should have complete knowledge and information of the field of investigation so that he can go in for correct planning and then implementation of the correct and effective methods for selection of the problem and then for solving it.

3. Qualification: The researcher should have a good back ground of study, which will enable the researcher to have a better knowledge and understanding of the subject.

4. Attitude: The researcher must have a vision of his own, an aim with some objectives to achieve something.

5. Should have an **open thinking.**

6. Should be **stable, having consistent thinking.**

7. Should **be honest, sincere, brave and ambitious.**

Q 6. METHODS OF RESEARCH

= Research is defined as the search for knowledge or any systematic investigation to establish facts.

Chrish Jordan.

Research means search for facts or ideas and to answer the questions in order to find a solution to the problem.

-Horton.

METHODS OF RESEARCH

There are three basic methods of research: 1. survey, 2. observation, and 3. experiment. Each method has its advantages and disadvantages.

1. **Experiment**
2. **Observation**
3. **Survey**

Survey

1. Survey is the most common method of gathering information in the social sciences.

2. It can be a face-to-face interview, telephone, mail, email, or web survey.

3. A personal interview is one of the best methods obtaining personal, detailed, or in-depth information.

4. It usually involves a lengthy questionnaire that the interviewer fills out while asking questions.

5. It allows for extensive probing by the interviewer and gives respondents the ability to elaborate their answers.

6. Telephone interviews are similar to face-to-face interviews.

7. They are more efficient in terms of time and cost, however, they are limited in the amount of in-depth probing that can be accomplished, and the amount of time that can be allocated to the interview.

8. A mail survey is more cost effective than interview methods.

9. The researcher can obtain opinions, but trying to meaningfully probe opinions is very difficult. Email and web

surveys are the most cost effective and fastest method.

Observation

1. The Observation research monitors respondents' actions without directly interacting with them.

2. It has been used for many years by A.C. Nielsen to monitor television viewing habits.

3. Psychologists often use one-way mirrors to study behavior.

4. Anthropologists and social scientists often study societal and group behaviors by simply observing them.

5. The fastest growing form of observation research has been made possible by the bar code scanners at cash registers, where purchasing habits of consumers can now be automatically monitored and summarized.

Experiment

1. In an experiment the investigator changes one or more variables over the course of the research

2. When all other variables are held constant (except the one being manipulated), changes in the dependent variable can be explained by the change in the independent variable.

3. It is usually very difficult to control all the variables in the environment.

Q 7. Types of research/ Classification of Research

= Research is defined as the search for knowledge or any systematic investigation to establish facts.

Chrish Jordan.

Research means search for facts or ideas and to answer the questions in order to find a solution to the problem.

-Horton.

Classification of Research

Research may be classified by purposes, i.e. it may be classified crudely according to its earnest desire directed towards or methods

I. According to earnest desire directed towards research may be classified as:

● Basic research Applied research

● Exploratory research Descriptive research

- Diagnostic research
- Evaluative research

Action research.

II. According to methods of study research may be classified as:

A. Qualitative research Phenomenological

- Grounded theory
- Historical
- Action research.

B. Quantitative research

I. Experimental

II. Non-experimental

I. **Experimental**

True experimental:

- Pre-test/post-test control group design
- Solomon four-group design
- Two group random sample design
- Matching sample design Factorial design.

- Quasi experimental:

- One-group pre-test/post-test design
- Non-randomized control group design Counter balanced design
- Time series design
- Control group time series design

II. Non-experimental Quantitative design

- Correlational design
- Descriptive design
- Time perspective design
- Retrospective design

- Prospective design
- Design that use existing data
- Focus group research
- Content analysis.

Research can be classified and discussed according **to their purposes and approaches as follows:**
A. Classification on the Basis of Purpose
1. Basic Research
It is also known as pure, theoretical or fundamental research, which is always aimed to enriching the theory by untravelling the untold mysteries of nature. It is a process in which data are scientifically collected to advance knowledge without particular reference to its immediate or practical use, which means, it advances scientific knowledge, regardless of whether knowledge is immediately usable or not.
2. Applied Research:
Applied research or empirical research always aims at enriching the application of the theory by discovering various new uses to which findings of basic research may be put and by showing limitations of these findings.
B. Classification on the Basis of Approaches
One the basis of approaches, research can be classified into two groups, i.e.,

i. **experimental approaches and**
ii. **non-experimental.**

i. Experimental Approaches
Experimental research is one in which the researcher makes changes in independent variables and studies their effects on dependent variables under controlled conditions.

Non experimental research is one in which the researcher simply measures the present level of the independent variable. For example, if a researcher wants to test the hypothesis, whether "increased autonomy of a job increases the level of satisfaction of nurses," he may carry this out in two ways.

I. First, he may take an existing job of nurse and redesign it to vary its levels of autonomy and see if there are concomitant variations in nurse's level of job satisfaction. This is conducting an experiment in which he actually manipulates autonomy-the study's independent variables

II. Second, he may look at incumbents in jobs that differed in terms of autonomy and see if jobs with greater autonomy have given greater level ofjob satisfaction to their incumbents. This is conducting a nonexperimental study. The following are some points of difference between these two types

CLASSIFICATION OF RESEARCH ACCORDING TO METHODS

Qualitative Research and Quantitative Research

Qualitative research is a systematic, interactive, subjective approach used to describe life experience and give them meaning.

Whereas quantitative research is a formal, objective systematic process to describe, test relationships, and examine cause and effect interaction among variables.

These two qualitative and quantitative approaches have emerged in recent years to develop nursing knowledge.

Quantitative research is based on the measurement of quantity or amount and it is applicable to phenomena that can be exposed in terms of quantity.

Qualitative research, on the other hand, is concerned with qualitative phenomena, is phenomena relating to or involving quality or kind

Pure research

1. Also called as the fundamental or the theoretical research.

2. Is basic and original.

3 Can lead to the discovery of a new theory.

4. Can result in the development or refinement of a theory that already exists.

5. Helps in getting knowledge without thinking formally of implementing it in practice based on the honesty, love and integrity of the researcher for discovering the truth

Applied research

1. Based on the concept of the pure research.

2. Is problem oriented?

3. Helps in finding results or solutions for real life problems.

4.Provides evidence of usefulness to society.

5. Helps in testing empirical content of a theory.

6. Utilizes and helps in developing the techniques that can be used for basic research.

8. Helps in testing the validity of a theory but under some conditions.

Provides data that can lead to the acceleration of the process of generalization.

Exploratory research

1. Involves exploring a general aspect.

2. Includes studying of a problem, about which nothing or a very little is known.

3. Follows a very formal approach of research.

4. Helps in exploring new ideas

. 5. Helps in gathering information to study a specific problem very minutely.

6. Helps in knowing the feasibility in attempting a study.

Descriptive research

1. Simplest form of research.

2. More specific in nature and working than exploratory research. .

3. It involves a mutual effort.

4. Helps in identifying various features of a problem.

5. Restricted to the problems that are describable and not arguable and the problems in which valid standards can be developed for standards.

6 Existing theories can be easily put under test by empirical observations.

7. Underlines factors that may lead to experimental research.

8. It consumes a lot of time.

9. It is not directed by hypothesis.

Diagnostic study

1. Quite similar to the descriptive research.

2. Identifies the causes of the problems and then solutions for this problems.

3. Related to causal relations.

4. it is directed by the hypothesis

5. Can be done only where knowledge is advanced.

Evaluation study

1. Form of applied research.

2. Studies the development project. 3.

3. Gives access to social or economical programmes.

4. Studies the quality and also the quantity of an activity.

Action research

1. Type of evaluation study.
2. Is a concurrent study.

Q.5. Definition of nursing research and scientific steps of nursing research .

= Definition of RESEARCH -

Nursing research is research that provides evidence used to support nursing practices. Nursing, as an evidence-based area of practice, has been developing since the time of Florence Nightingale to the present day,

where many nurses now work as researchers based in universities as well as in the health care setting.

Steps Of Scientific Research.

I. Identifying the problem: It is a clear finding of the problem that should be studied. In general broad topic area is selected and then the topic is narrowed down to a specific one. It may be from personal experiences or literature sources.

II. Review of literature: It is one of the most important step in the research process. A literature review is an account of what has been already established or published on a particular research topic by various researchers.

III. Developing the a theoretical/conceptual framework : It is the valuable part of scientific research. Which helps in

the selection of the study characters and in defining them. It also directs to the prediction and the interpretation of the study findings.

IV. Identifying the study Assumptions : Assumptions are held to be true but have not necessarily seen proven. It influences the questions that are asked. It is based on the information collected and study interpretation.

V. Developing the a theoretical/conceptual framework : It is the valuable part of scientific research. Which helps in the selection of the study characters and in defining them. It also directs to the prediction and the interpretation of the study findings.

VI. Identifying the study Assumptions : Assumptions are held to be true but have not necessarily seen proven. It influences the questions that are asked. It is based on the information collected and study interpretation.

VII. Formulating the Hypothesis or Research Question: Hypothesis predicts the relationship between two or more characters. According to the asked questions in the problem statement. The hypothesis furnishes the answer to it. It is testable or verifiable by the information gathered. The research is guided by research questions that are further elaboration of the problem statement.

VIII. Selecting the research Design : It is the plan for how the study will be conducted as well as concerned with the type of information that will be collected.

IX. Identifying the population/sample: The population means the complete set of individuals or objects that posses some common characteristics of interest to the researcher. The subgroup of populations is called study sample.

X. Conducting a pilot study : A pilot study is a miniature trial version of the planned study. It reveals the feasibility of the study and helps to test the instruments. It also plays a role in gaining experience with the study process and it indicates that where the revision should be made.

XI. Collecting Data : It is the process of collection or gathering of pieces of information's facts that are related to the study.

XII. Organizing the data for Analysis : It is the grouping of information's for tabulation and evaluation purpose. A statistician should be consulted in the early and phase of the research process. The statistician can help to follow the appropriate analytical method.

XIII. Interpreting the findings : After the data are analyzed the finding of the result are compared with those of previous studies for further recommendation.

CHAPTER TWO

Nursing Research.

Q 1. Define Nursing Research.
= DEFINITION
1. American nurses association:
Nursing research develops knowledge about health and promotion of health over the full life span, care of persons with health problems and disabilities and nursing actions to enhance the ability of individuals to **respond effectively to actual or potential health problems.**
2. International nurses (Benolie) 1984:
Nursing research supports the need for nursing research as a means of improving health and welfare of the people. Nursing research is a way to identify new knowledge, improve professional educational practice and use of resources effectively.
3. International council of nurses (1986):
nursing research is a way to identify new knowledge, improve professional education and practices and use of resources effectively.
4. Commission of nursing research (1981):
nursing research is defined as the application of scientific inquiry to the phenomena of concern to nursing. Nursing research seeks to find new knowledge that can eventually be applied in providing nursing care to patients.
5 . Walls and Bauzell (1981):
nursing research to the use of systematic, controlled, empirical and critical investigation in attempting to discover or confirm facts

that relate to specific problem or questions about the practice of nursing.

6. Polit and Hungler (1995):

Nursing research is a systematic search for knowledge about issue of importance in the nursing profession.

Q 2. Goal of nursing research

= 1. American nurses association:

Nursing research develops knowledge about health and promotion of health over the full life span, care of persons with health problems and disabilities and nursing actions to enhance the ability of individuals to **respond effectively to actual or potential health problems.**

2. Polit and Hungler (1995):

Nursing research is a systematic search for knowledge about issue of importance in the nursing profession.

Goals of nursing research

1. Build a body of nursing knowledge.

2. improve nursing care

3. improve patient care outcomes

4. Improve quality of life

5. Define and expand the scope of nursing practice

6 .Validate improvements in nursing

Make healthcare efficient and cost effective.

Q 3. CHARACTERISTICS OF NURSING RESEARCH

=1. American nurses association:

Nursing research develops knowledge about health and promotion of health over the full life span, care of persons with health problems and disabilities and nursing actions to enhance the ability of individuals to **respond effectively to actual or potential health problems.**

2. Polit and Hungler (1995):

Nursing research is a systematic search for knowledge about issue of importance in the nursing profession.

CHARACTERISTICS OF NURSING RESEARCH

1. Research discrete towards the solution of a problem.

2. Research emphasizing the development of generalizations of principles or theories. Research is more than information retrieval (i.e.) the simple gathering of information's.

3. Research based upon observable experience or empirical evidence. Research rejects revelation methods of establishing knowledge and accepts only what can be verified by observation.

4. Research demands accurate observation and description.

5. Research gathering new data from primary or firsthand source or existing data for a new purpose.

6. Research carefully designed.

7. Research requiring expertise.

8. Research striving to be objective and logical.

9. Research monitoring the quest for answer to solve the problems.

10. Research characterized by patience and unhurried activity.

11. Research carefully recorded and reported.

12. Research some time requires courage.

Q 4. NEED OF RESEARCH IN NURSING

= 1. American nurses association:

Nursing research develops knowledge about health and promotion of health over the full life span, care of persons with health problems and disabilities and nursing actions to enhance the ability of individuals to **respond effectively to actual or potential health problems.**

2. Polit and Hungler (1995):

Nursing research is a systematic search for knowledge about issue of importance in the nursing profession.

NEED OF RESEARCH IN NURSING

The Ultimate goal of any profession is to provide its clients with maximum effective and efficient services. A profession seeks to improve the practice of its members and to enhance its professional stature. For the continual development of a relevant body of knowledge. Nursing research represents a critically important 'tool' for the nursing Profession to acquire such knowledge.

Need of research in nursing

1. To maintain the professionalism, ie: professional dignity

2. To haveautonomy in nursing.

3. To have accountability

4. To develop critical thinking, creativity, and problem solving technique.

5. To develop new technique of nursing intervention.

6. To evaluate the effectiveness of new nursing techniques.

7. To develop a scientific body of knowledge

8. To answer problem relating to health delivery and care

8.To determineareas of need relating to education, IPR and patient teaching.

Fig. 2.8 : Need for Nursing Research

NEED OF RESEARCH IN NURSING

1. Professionalism: Nurses increasingly recognize the need to extend the base of nursing knowledge as part of professional responsibility and endorse research investigations as a way to achieve this objective. Moreover nurses are committed to the evolution of a fairly distinct body of knowledge that separates nursing from other profession. Nursing is only one of the several professions involved in the delivery of health care. Information from nursing investigation helps to define better the unique role that nursing plays.

2. Accountability: During the 1970's nursing leaders pointed out that the quality of nursing care cannot be improved until information based accountability becomes as much part of nursing tradition as humanitarianism. Nurses who corporate research evidence into their clinical decisions are being professionally accountable to their clients and are also helping nursing to achieve its own professional identity.

3. Social relevance of nursing: Nurses today are being asked more than ever before to document their role in the delivery of health services. People are recognizing health care as a right rather than a privilege and with spiraling costs, are asking various groups of health professionals how their service contribute to the total delivery of health care. This increased interest in examining health care practices makes it essential for nurses to evaluate the efficacy of their practices and to modify or abandon those practices shown to have no effect on client health.

Q 5. **ROLE OF NURSE IN RESEARCH**

=**1. American nurses association:**

Nursing research develops knowledge about health and promotion of health over the full life span, care of persons with health problems and disabilities and nursing actions to enhance the ability of individuals to **respond effectively to actual or potential health problems.**

2. Polit and Hungler (1995):

Nursing research is a systematic search for knowledge about issue of importance in the nursing profession.

ROLE OF NURSE IN RESEARCH

Nurses act as principal investigators, members of research teams, identifiers of researchable problems, evaluators of research findings, users of research findings, client advocates during studies, and subjects/ participants in research. Research utilization focuses on the implementation of findings from specific research studies.

1. Principal Investigator: Nurses can and should serve as principal investigators in scientific investigations. To be a principal investigator, special research preparation is necessary.

2. Members of a research team: Nurses may act as data collectors or administer the experimental intervention of the study. As Nurses increasingly participate in research, it is possible that interest and enthusiasm to conduct their own investigations may grow.

3. Evaluator of research findings: all nurses should be involved in the evaluation of research findings. As research consumers, nurses have the obligation to become familiar with research findings and determine the usefulness of these findings in the practice area. The evaluation of research is not an easy task.

4. User of research findings: After evaluating research findings, nurses should use relevant finding in their practice. The primary goal of nursing research, as has been mentioned, is the improved care of clients. However, nurses must be judicious in their use of research findings.

5. Client advocate during studies: nurses have the responsibility to act as client advocates when clients are involved in research. Nurses can help answer questions and explain a study to potential participants before the study begins. They also can be available during the study to **answer questions or provide support to study participants.**

6. Subject in studies: Nurses also can act as subjects in research. Many nurses are involved in a long-term survey study that is being conducted by researcher at Harvard Medical School, with funds provided by the National Institute of health.

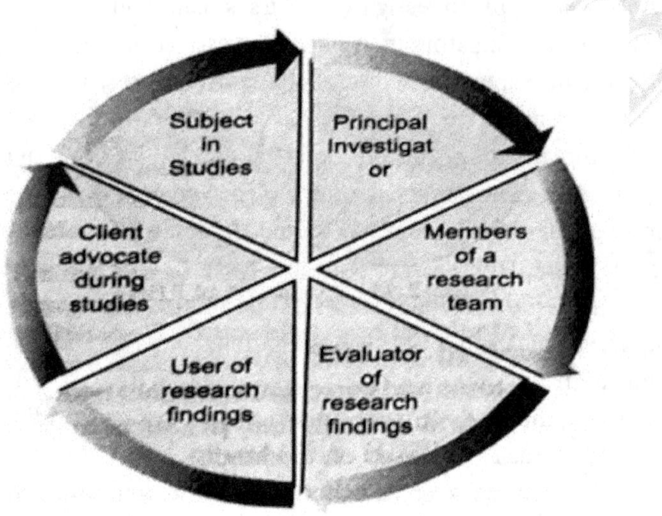

Fig. 2.9 : Role of nurse in research

ROLE OF NURSE IN RESEARCH

Q 7. EVIDENCE BASED NURSING RESEARCH
= American nurses association:

Nursing research develops knowledge about health and promotion of health over the full life span, care of persons with health problems and disabilities and nursing actions to enhance the ability of individuals to **respond effectively to actual or potential health problems.**

EVIDENCE BASED NURSING RESEARCH

Evidence based nursing practice was started in 1800s with Florence nightingale.

it is a problem solving approach to clinical decision making. It is the process of integrating clinical knowledge, judgment, proficiency skills with the best available clinical evidence, such as nursing practice into patient care.

Gaining knowledge and skills in evidence based practice provides nurses and other clinicians the tools needed to take ownership of their practice and transform health care in a comprehensive manner.

Definition:

1. Evidence based practice is an integration of the best evidence available, nursing expertise and the values gritand preferences of the individuals, families and communities are served-**Chris Jordan.**

2. Evidence based practice is a continuous interactive process involving the explicit, conscientious and judicious consideration of the best available evidence to provide care. **Canadian nurses association.**

3. Evidence based practice is the conscientious use of current best evidence in making clinical decisions about patient care.

Evidence-based nursing practice (EBNP)

1. It means that nurses make clinical decisions based on the best research evidence, their clinical expertise, and the health care preferences of their patients/clients.

2. Although EBNP may be based on factors research findings, such as patient preferences and the expertise of clinicians, the aim of EBNP is to provide the best possible care based on the best available research

Purposes of EBP

1. To provide the highest quality and most cost-efficient nursing care possible.

2. To advance quality of care provided by the nurses.

3. To increase satisfaction of patients.

4. To focus on nursing practice away from habits and tradition to evidence and research.

Steps involved in EBP

1. Select a topic and correct appropriate reviews.

2. Analyze data for clinical practice and design interventions based on evidence.

3. Predict and analyze outcomes and examine the pattern of behavior and outcomes.

4. Identify gaps in EBP and evaluate projects to determine and implement best practices.

Limitations

1. Resistant to change in nursing practice.

2. Ability to critically appraise research findings in nursing

3. Poor administrative support in nursing.

4. Fear of stepping on ones toes in nursing

5. lack of continuing eduction programmes in nursing.

Q8. Explain the problems faced in nursing research

=

PROBLEMS IN NURSING, HEALTH, AND SOCIAL RESEARCH

Research is not an easy activity in itself. Moreover, it becomes more difficult when it is conducted outside the laboratory. Research in health, nursing, and social sciences is usually carried out in natural , where the researcher faces the following main problems:

☐ **Fallibility of disciplined research:** Indeed most of the research studies in the field of nursing, health, and social sciences have some limitations. Each research question can be solved by different approaches, depending on several factors. Therefore, it is always confusing to decide a best approach for solving a research question. It means that in these disciplines, none of the approaches can solve a question completely. However, repeated attempts to solve a similar question with identical answers may increase the value of generated evidences.

Handling multiple variables: Most of the research studies in the field of nursing and health and social sciences usually focus on the measurements of the multiple variables in single attempt. This attempt of handling multiple data in single instance not only causes the data collection, analysis, and interpretation problems, but also needs lots of time, energy, and money to handle these multiple nonnumerical data.

Difficulty in control on external variables: Research in nursing, health, and social sciences is usually conducted in natural settings. Therefore, it becomes very difficult to exert control over external variables while measuring the effect of independent variable on dependent variable. For instance, a researcher wants to assess the efficacy of an antibiotic in treatment of an infection where patient's biochemical parameters, diet, lifestyle, consumption of other drugs, etc. are the external variables, which are ethically difficult to control.

Minimal possibility of laboratory research: Research in nursing, health, and social sciences usually deals with phenomena related to humans, where ethically as well practically it becomes very difficult to conduct research studies in laboratory. Most of the researches in these disciplines are conducted outside laboratory, in natural settings..

Lack of standardized tools: Research in nursing, health, and social sciences deals with natural phenomena where valid and reliable standardized tools are needed to generate empirical evidences. However, it is evident that there is significant lack of valid and reliable tools to measure variables in nursing, health, and social science disciplines.

Measuring qualitative phenomenon through quantitative means: It is usually observed that several phenomena in field of nursing, health, and social sciences are qualitative in nature. However, it can be commonly seen that these disciplines usually measure these qualitative phenomena by using quantitative means where effectiveness of evidence get distorted. This is assumed that this usually happens because of the superficial knowledge of qualitative research among professionals of nursing, health, and social sciences.

Lack of interest among researchers: It is generally observed that people in the field of nursing, health, and social sciences conduct research studies only for specific purposes such as a partial fulfilment of a particular degree or due to a specific compulsion as a part of their job. However, it is generally observed that professionals in field of nursing, health, and social sciences experience lack of interest because of several reasons like lack of government funding, research training, and motivation.

Ethical constraints: Research studies in nursing, health, and social sciences deal with human beings where safeguarding their rights become an important issue. Moreover, several problems cannot be studied only because of the ethical constraints.

Lack of qualitative research expertise: Qualitative research methods are considered to be best to study phenomena in the field of nursing, health, and social sciences but there is a significant dearth of experts equipped with the knowledge of qualitative research.

Q 9. LIMITATIONS IN RESEARCH

= Limitations of a dissertation are potential weaknesses in the study that are mostly out of your control, given limited funding, choice of research design, statistical model constraints, or other factors. In addition, a limitation is a restriction on the study that cannot be reasonably dismissed and can affect your design and results.

Meaning:

1. Limitations are conditions that restrict thescope of study or may affect the outcome and cannot be controlled by the researcher.
2. Knowledge of limitations must always be balanced with the likely benefits of the outcome of an enquiry.

3. All research studies also have limitations and a finite scope.

4. Limitations are often imposed by time, budget, legal and ethical constraints and reliability of the data.

5. Accurate up-to-date information obtained by research can be of enormous value to the society in gaining and maintain it competitive edge.

Types of limitations:

1. **Budgetary constraints**: Gathering and processing data can be very expensive. Many researchers may lack the expertise to conduct extensive surveys to gather primary data

2. **Time constraints:**The data gathering and processing may be time consuming. May researchers may lack time to conduct an extensive survey within the available time to complete their requirement.

3. Reliability of the data: The value of any research finding depends critically on the accuracy of the data collected. Data quality can be compromised via a number of potential routes. For example leading questions, unrepresentative samples, biased interviewers etc. efforts to ensure that data is accurate, samples are representative and interviewers are objective will all add to the costs of the research, but such costs are necessary if poor decisions and expensive mistakes are to be avoided.

4. Legal and ethical constraints: The researcher must ensure that while gathering the data should ensure that the data they obtain is kept secure and is only kept for as log as it is necessary. It must be made clear as to why data is being collected and the consent of participants is obtained.

Q 10 Discuss the importance of clinical researches in nursing.
= Health research serves two major purposes:

1. First basic research is necessary to generate new knowledge and technologies to deal with major unresolved health problems.
2. Second, applied research is necessary to identify priority problems and to design and evaluate policies and programmes that will deliver the greatest health benefits, making optimal use of available resources.

- In addition to providing and coordinating clinical care, clinical research nurses have a central role in assuring participant safety, maintenance of informed consent, integrity of protocol implementation, accuracy of data collection and recording, and appropriate follow up.
- Nursing care provided to research participants is driven by study requirements and the collection of research data as well as clinical indications.
- Patient assessment and clinical data collection may include clinical observations, clinical measurements, specimen collection and preparation, and documentation of research participant reported outcomes.

- Interventions and study procedures may include administration of investigational drugs, performance of an experimental or investigational surgical or radiological procedure, detailed clinical evaluation or phenotyping to characterize the natural history and etiology of a disease, or delivery of a psychosocial intervention.
- The participant's response to the study intervention may make additional nursing care necessary. These care requirements range from educating the participant about self-monitoring to comprehensive physiological monitoring and life support in an intensive care unit.
- Clinical Research allows you to acquire skills and techniques to be capable to collaborate efficiently with co-workers in basic sciences and other disciplines in the successful conduct of high-quality clinical trials

Clinical Research helps develop proficiency in the study design exhibiting the dept. and difficulty of clinical and translational science applications

Clinical research allows you to understand how to perform and control clinical research

Clinical research allows you to gain knowledge about various regulatory authorities and their specification to approve marketing of healthcare products.

Gaining knowledge of the use of medical data, data evaluation and use of data databased

CHAPTER THREE

Research Process.

Q 1. Define research process

= **RESEARCH PROCESS**

1. Scientific research involves a systematic process that focuses on being objective and gathering a multitude of information for analysis so that the researcher can come to a conclusion.

2. This process is used in all research and evaluation projects, regardless of the research method (scientific method of inquiry, evaluation research, or action research)

Q2. STEPS IN NURSING RESEARCH PROCESS / RESEARCH PROCESS

= **RESEARCH PROCESS**

1. Scientific research involves a systematic process that focuses on being objective and gathering a multitude of information for analysis so that the researcher can come to a conclusion.

2. This process is used in all research and evaluation projects, regardless of the research method (scientific method of inquiry, evaluation research, or action research)

STEPS IN NURSING RESEARCH PROCESS

The phases and steps in the research project gives an overview of the research process. Actually, there were five basic phases involved in conducting research, i.e. assessment, diagnosis, planning, implementation and evaluation.

1. In assessment phase, the investigators select the topic and identifies a research problems, formulates the proposal for research project, reviews the literature, concerning the project and defines the concepts and variable to be studied.

2. In diagnosis phase, the investigator states the hypothesis, examines the possible ethical implications of the research proposal, and reviews pertinent literature and also identifies the theory, assumptions and limitations of the proposal.

3. In planning phase, the researcher describes the research design and methods of research including sampling, data collection, instruments to be used and method of data analysis, obtains informed consent from subjects to be studied in the pilot study, conducts the study, and revises proposals in the light of findings, and plans how to communicate findings.

4. In implementing phase, the researcher collects data from the subjects.

5. In evaluation phase, the investigator performs analyses and interpretation of the data collected from the target population and communicates the findings as per plan made in the planning phase.

The brief explanation of these five phases indicates that in each phase, the researcher has to follow different steps. Each phase may be divided into various steps that may differ in some ways from project to project. The common steps of each phase will now be examined.

Research process consists of phases or steps that can be compared and contrasted with those of the nursing process.

1. Identify the problem: the first step and one of the most important steps in the research process is to clearly identify the problem that will be studied. This step of research process may be most difficult of all and may take a great deal of time. Study problem can be identified from personal experiences, from literature sources, from previous research or through the testing of theories.

2. Determine the purpose of the study: there must be a sound rational or justification for every research project. Some studies viewed as inconsequential and wasteful of time and money. The research must take explicit the expectations for the use of the study results. If the purpose of a study is clearly presented and justified, the research will be much more likely to receive approval for the study and also will be more likely to obtain subjects for the study.

3. Review the literature: research should build on previous knowledge. Before beginning a study, it is important to determine what knowledge exists of the study topic. A thorough literature review provides a foundation on which to base new knowledge and generally is conducted well before any data are collected in quantitative study.

Identify the problem

- Determine the purpose of the study
- Review the literature
- Develop a theoretical/conceptual frame work
- Identify the study assumptions Knowledge the limitation of the study

Formulate the hypothesis

- Define study variables/terms Select the research design
- Identify the population
- Select the sample

Conduct a pilot study

- Collect the data
- Organize the data for analysis
- Analyze the data
- Organize the data for analysis Analyze the data
- Interpret the findings
- Communicating the findings

4. Develop a theoretical / conceptual frame work: a theory is a systematic vision of reality that serves a scientific purpose. Research and theory are interview Research can test theories as well as help to develop and refine theories. The theoretical or conceptual frame work will assist in selection of the study variables and identifying them. The frame work provides the prospective from which the investigator views the problem and is not merely 'restatement of previous research but an integration of the existing theoretical traditions and knowledge about the topic_

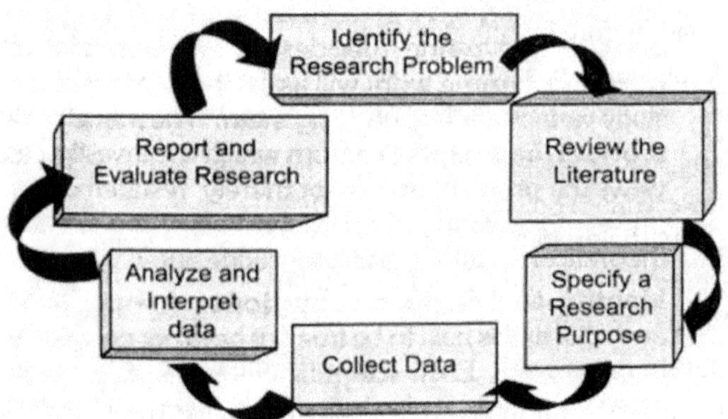

Flow Chart - 3.1 : The process of research

STEPS IN NURSING RESEARCH PROCESS

5. Identify the study assumptions: Assumptions are belief that is held to be true but have not necessarily been proven. Each scientific investigation is based on assumption. It also influences the questions that are asked, the data that are gathered, the methods used data. to gather the data and the interpretation of the

6. Knowledge the limitation of the study: the researcher should try to identify study limitations or weaknesses. Limitations are uncontrolled variables that may affect study results and limit the generalizability of the findings. The research should openly acknowledge the limitations of a study, as much as possible, before data are collected.

7. Formulate hypothesis: a hypothesis predicts the relationship between two or more variables. Hypothesis in other words, is a prediction ofexpected out comes, it states the relationships the researcher aspects to find as a result of the study.

8. Define study variables / terms: the definitions are usually dictionary definitions or theoretical definitions, a variable should be operationally defined. An operational definition indicates how a variable will be observed or measured. Operation definitions frequently include the instrument that will be used to measure the variables.

9. Select the research design: it is concerned with the type of data that will be collected and means used to obtain these data. For e.g., the researcher must decide if the study will examine cause and effect relationship or will only describe existing situations. Research design can be categorized as quantitative or qualitative. They also can be categorized as experimental or non experimental. Experimental design can be further divided into true experimental, quasi-experimental and pre-experimental designs. Non experimental designs include survey studies, correlation studies, comparative studies and methodological studies.

10. Identify the population: the researcher must specify the broad population or group interest as well as the actual population and the second type is called the accessible population. The researcher would like to assert that study results apply to a wide target population, this population must be similar to the accessible population for such an assertion to be made.

11. Select the sample: the sample is chosen to represent the population and is used to make generation about the population. The method of selecting the sample will determine how representative the sample is of the population. The researcher must make the determination of which sampling method to use, after considering the advantages and disadvantages of the various type of probability and non-probability sampling method.

12. Conduct a pilot study: a pilot study involves a miniature, trial version of the planned study. People are selected for the pilot study who are similar in characteristics to the sample that will be used for the actual study. The function of pilot study is to obtain information for improving the project or for assessing its feasibility.

13.Collect the data: the researcher should plan typically specifies procedures for collecting data for describing the study to the subjects, for obtaining the necessary informed consents, and if necessary for training those who will be involved in the collection of the data. Although the data collection step of the research may be very time consuming, it is sometimes considered to be the most exciting part of **research.**

14. Organize the data for analysis: the researcher should have prepared dummy tables and graphs that could be filled in with the data once they are obtained. A statistician should be consulted in the early phase of the research process. As well as in the data analysis phase of the study.

15. Analyze the data: statistical analysis cover a broad range oftechniques, including some simple procedures as well as complex and sophisticated methods. Now, a researcher can sit at a computer terminal and input large amounts of data and receive the results of the analysis almost instantaneously.

16. Interpret the findings: before the results of a study can be communicated effectively, they must be organized and interpreted in a systematic fashion. Interpre tion refers to the process of making sense of the results and examining the implications of the findings within a broader context.

17. Communicating the findings: the final step in the research process and the most important one for nursing is the communication of the study findings. Research findings can be communicated through many different mediums. The best method of reaching large number of nurses is through publication in research journals.

Q 3. Explain the role of nurse in research process

= RESEARCH PROCESS

1. Scientific research involves a systematic process that focuses on being objective and gathering a multitude of information for analysis so that the researcher can come to a conclusion.

2. This process is used in all research and evaluation projects, regardless of the research method (scientific method of inquiry, evaluation research, or action research)

ROLE OF NURSE IN RESEARCH PROCESS

1. Many nurses have expressed an interest in conducting a nursing research project, but some have not had sufficient or recent

exposure to the process of how to develop a research study.

2. The nursing research process can be outlined using the nursing process steps of assessment, planning, intervention and evaluation.

3. In the assessment phase the problem is identified, the literature is reviewed, and the variables are identified.

4. In the planning phase the research question or hypothesis is formulated, and decisions are made on how the variables will be measured and how the sample will be chosen.

5. In the intervention phase the data collection occurs; in the evaluation phase the data is analyzed and interpreted and the findings are communicated.

6. By giving nurses a detailed yet understandable plan on how to conduct nursing research, their curiosity is encouraged and the body of knowledge will grow.

CHAPTER FOUR

Ethics in Nursing Research

Q 1. ETHICAL PRINCIPLES OF RESEARCH
= ETHICAL PRINCIPLES OF RESEARCH

Honesty: Strive for honesty in all scientific communications. Honestly report data, results, methods and procedures, and publication status. Do not fabricate, falsify, or misrepresent data. Do not deceive colleagues, research sponsors, or the public.

Objectivity: Strive to avoid bias in experimental design, data analysis, data interpretation, peer review, personnel decisions, grant writing, expert testimony, and other aspects of research where objectivity is expected or required. Avoid or minimize bias or self deception. Disclose personal or financial interests that may affect research.

Integrity: Keep your promises and agreements; act with sincerity; strive for consistency of thought and action.

Carefulness: Avoid careless errors and negligence; carefully and critically examine your own work and the work of your peers. Keep good records of research activities, such as data collection, research design, and correspondence with agencies or journals.

Openness: Share data, results, ideas, tools, resources. Be open to criticism and new ideas.

Respect for Intellectual Property: Honor patents, copyrights, and other forms of intellectual property. Do not use unpublished data, methods, or results without permission. Give proper acknowledgement or credit for all contributions to research. Never plagiarize.

Confidentiality: Protect confidential communications, such as papers or grants submitted for publication, personnel records, trade or military secrets, and patient records.

Responsible Publication: Publish in order to advance research and scholarship, not to advance just your own career. Avoid wasteful and duplicative publication.

Responsible Mentoring: Help to educate, mentor, and advise students. Promote their welfare and allow them to make their own decisions.

CHAPTER FIVE

Research Problem

Q1. Define Research Problem .

= Define

1. Research problem is defined as a situation for which we have no ready and successful response by instinct or by previous acquired habit. We must find out what to do. i.e., the solution can be found out only after an investigation -**R.S. Woodworth.**

2. A problem is an interrogative sentence or statement that asks what relation exists between two or more variables. The answer to questions will provide what is having sought in the research. **–Kerlinger.**

3. **According to Marilynn J. Wood:** the research problem is the full exposition of the idea that you want to study.

Q 2. Factors Involves in Selecting Research Problem

=1. Research problem is defined as a situation for which we have no ready and successful response by instinct or by previous acquired habit. We must find out what to do. i.e., the solution can be found out only after an investigation -**R.S. Woodworth.**

2. **According to Marilynn J. Wood:** the research problem is the full exposition of the idea that you want to study.

Interest

Interest should be the most important consideration in selecting a research problem. A research endeavor is usually time consuming and involves hard work and possibly unforeseen problems.

Magnitude The researcher should have sufficient knowledge about the research process to be able to visualize the work involved in completing the proposed study. Narrow the topic down to something manageable, specific and clear. It is extremely important to select a topic that the research can manage within the time and resources.

Measurement of subjects

If the research using concepts, make sure that the concepts are clear about its indicators and their measurements. If the researcher plan to measure the effectiveness of early ambulation after surgery, he must be clear as to what determines effectiveness and how it will be measured.

Level of expertise

The research should make sure that he has an adequate level of expertise for the task proposing. Allow for the fact that the researcher will learn during the study may receive help from the research supervises and others.

Relevance: Select a topic that is of relevance to the researcher as a professional. Ensure that the research study adds to the existing body of knowledge, bridges current gaps or is useful in policy formation.

Availability of data

If the research topic entails collection of information from secondary sources (office records, client records, census or other already-published reports etc) before finalizing the topic make sure that these data's are available and in the format the researcher want.

Ethical issues

Another important consideration in formatting a research problem is the ethical issues involved. In the course of conducting a research study, the study population may be adversely affected by some of the questions (directly or indirectly) deprived of an intervention, expected to share sensitive and private information. How ethical issues can affect the study population and how ethical problems can be overcome should be thoroughly examined at the problem formulation stage.

Q 3.Define variable and Explain types of variables

= Definition:

1. A variable is a concept or abstract idea that can be described in measurable terms. In research, this term refers to the measurable characteristics, qualities, traits, or attributes of a particular individual, object, or situation being studied.

2. Variables are properties or characteristics of some event, object, or person that can take on different values or amounts.

3. Variables are things that we measure, control, of manipulate in research. They differ in many respects, most notably in the role they are given in our research and in the type of measures that can be applied to them.

1. The independent variable :

Is that phenomenon in the hypothesis that, in the experimental study to test, the hypothesis, is not manipulated by the investigator. It is also called the cause, stimulus, experimental variable or treatment, the variable that is manipulated by the researcher, in order to study the effect upon the dependent variable.

2. The dependent variable:

Is that phenomenon in the hypothesis that, in the experimental study, to test the hypothesis, is not manipulated, but is accepted as € Disease it occurs. It is also called the effect, the response, the criterion measure; behavior or outcome that is researcher wishes to predict, study, explain.

1. **Extraneous variables:**

Are all variables in a hypothesis testing investigation that are not dependent variable jar criterion measures of the dependent variables. That means all those variables present in research environment especially in research involving human subjects that may interfere with the research findings, by acting as unwanted independent variables and confusing the results of the research.

4. Intervening variables:

They intervene between cause and effect. It is difficult to observe, as they are related with individuals feelings such as boredom, fatigue excitement At times some of these variables cannot be controlled or measured but have an important effect upon the result of the study as it intervenes between cause and effect. Though difficult, it has to be controlled through appropriate design. E.g. "Effect of immediate reinforcement on learning the parts of speech".

5. The accounted for variables :

Are those variables about which, observations are gathered during the study for the sake of additional information they will provide, but which actually are not needed in relation to testing the hypothesis

6. Controlled for variables:

Are those extraneous variables that are apt to affect the dependent variable in a manner similar to the dependent variable in manner similar to effect of the independent variable.

7. Confounding variables

are extraneous variables that influence the dependent variables in the same way the independent variable influences it. These are those who would class confounding variables as those of programme concern, after the independent and dependent variables. It will be noted, however, that, if variables that are apt to confound the findings are controlled for, there will be no confounding variables. Their confounding influence will have to be precluded from occurring. When speaking of relationships between variables, the researcher is essentially asking Is X related to Y? What is the effect of X on Y? How are X1 and X2 related to Y? The researcher asking a question about the relationship between one or more independent variables and dependent variable.

Q4. Enlist the Sources of Problem Statements.

= Previous Research

The critical appraisal of research studies that appear in journals may indirectly suggest problem area by stimulating the readers thinking. The organized body of nursing knowledge contains information about previous research. The investigator may have read something that did not make sense or work as predicted. A nurse may have read variety of studies and wonder which findings are most valid. For example, studies related to cost effectiveness.

Popular Conceptions

While taking care of health, certain traditional practices have been practiced according to their cultural belief or certain old practices of the new world. To test these practices, researcher may get an idea for conducting study. These researchers challenged a popular belief and found evidence that contraindicate the belief. Numerous beliefs guide nursing practice, and they need to be examined through research.

Empirical Interest

The sudden insight, which may arise from seeing things in a different way, is another source of research problems. Sudden awareness of something that has not been noticed before is another source of nursing research. (Curiosity about every day clinical practice is a rich source for nursing research).

Practical Needs

Clinical practice provides a wealth of experience from which research problems can be derived. The nurse may observe the occurrence of particular event or pattern and become curious about why it occurs as well as its relationships to other factors, in the client/patient environment. For example, OPD patients on treatment getting severe dispend (may be due to anxiety). And in clinical area, a nurse may find an ideal answer to any question may be a practical need for nursing may be source for research problem.

Political Concerns

The political climate, which places emphasis on constraining health-care cost, cause and effect of treatment of diseases and improving the standards of health, and implementation of vertical health programmers, has provided many avenues for research.

Priorities

There are so many problems emerging in providing health care services to reach the preserved people. Various groups, within nursing have identified priorities for nursing research that if followed could result in the creation of knowledge that nurses need to care for future generations. The lists of priorities can serve source of research problems for the nurse investigator.

Priorities for nursing research also have been set for some nursing specialty areas, e.g. Nursing Service, Nursing Administration, Nursing Education, Medical surgical Nursing, Pediatric Nursing, Psychiatric Nursing, Community Health Nursing etc.

Interested in Untested Theory

Verification of an untested nursing theory provides a relatively uncharted territory from which research problems can be derived. In as much as theories themselves are not tested, a researcher

Interest of Professional Organization

Researchable problems also are generated by professional organization priorities and quality, improvement issues. An example, such organization will include Trained Nurses association Govt. Nurses Association of Karnataka and others.

Q.14. Sources of Research Problem.

= The common sources from which a researcher may find ideas to identify and formulate a research problem include

Personal experiences:

Day-to-day personal experience of a researcher may serve as good source of ideas to formulate a research problem.

For example, a researcher observed domestic violence suffered by wives of alcoholic husbands. This experience may

provide ideas to identify several research problems related to domestic violence against women. There may be so

many such life experiences of a researcher which could be used to develop a research problem.

• Practical experience:

Nurses get plenty of ideas to formulate research problems from their clinical experiences. Every curious nurse has several questions to be answered that are encountered during clinical experience. For example, a nurse finds that

unrestricted visiting hours in surgical wards reduced the analgesic demand among postoperative patients. In another instance, a nurse observed that application of ice at the site of heparin injection reduced the chances of ecchymosis. Such clinical experiences could be rich sources of ideas to identify a significant research problem.

• Critical appraisal of literature:

When we critically study books and articles relating to the subject of our interest, including research reports, opinion articles, and summaries of clinical issues, pertinent questions may arise in our mind. These may strike reader's mind

indirectly by stimulating imagination and directly by stating what additional research is needed.

For example, a nurse reads an article on the prevalence of the pin site infection among patients with external

fixators. While reading this article, she learns that there is lack of con sensus about pin site care. This information may serve as a basis to formulate a research problem.

Another type of literature that acts as a source of good research ideas is the requests for proposals (RFPs) that are

published by government agencies and some companies. Typically, the RFPs describe the problems that need addressing, the contexts in which theyoperate, the approach they would like you to take to investigate and to address the problem, and the amount they would be willing to pay for such research.

• Previous research:

A body of knowledge should be developed on a sound foundation of re search findings. Usually, at the end of a research, further research problems are suggested, based on the shortcomings of previous research, which can be investigated. In nursing profession, not much research has been yet done; therefore, this profession needs researchers who are willing to replicate or repeat other studies on different samples and settings where all the essential elements of the original study are held intact. Further refinements may be made in the experimental treatments, or more appropriate outcome measures may be identified.

• Existing theories:

Research is a process of theory development and theory testing Nurses use many theories from other disciplines in

their practices. If an existing theory is used in developing a researchable problem, a specific statement from the theory must be isolated. Generally, a part or parts of the theory are subjected to testing in the clinical situation. The testing of an existing theory is definitely needed in nursing; therefore, they serve as good sources of research problems.

• Consumer feedback:

Research problems may be generated from the results of activities aimed to solicit patient feedback. For example, at

the time of discharge of patient after angiography, a nurse obtained a feedback from the patient. Patient verbalized that it was a wonderful experience except discomfort during removal of pressure dressing at the femoral puncture site. This feedback provided a concept for nurse to research on efficacy of available alternative means of dressing at puncture site to minimize the discomfort among patient undergoing angiography. *Performance improvement

activities: The performance improvement activities, known as quality improvement activities, are used to improve processes and outcomes t meet regulatory requirement. In the process of performance activities, several issues in

merge that require answers through research. Thus performance improvement activity also serve as an important source of research problem.

• Social issues:

Sometimes, topics are suggested by more global contemporary social or political ues of relevance to the health care community. For example, HIV/AIDS, female feticade sexual harassment, domestic violence, and gender equality in

health care and in earth a some of the current social and political issues of concern for health care professionals. An ide for a study may stem from a familiarity with social concerns or controversial social issues.

***Brainstorming:**

Brainstorming sessions are good techniques to find new questions, when an intensified discussion among interested

people of the profession is conducted to find more ideas to formulate a good research problem. For example, ideas

for studies may emerge from reviewing research priorities by having brainstorming session with othe nurses,

researchers, or nursing faculty.

***Intuition:**

Traditionally, intuitions are considered good sources of knowledge as well a sources to find new research problems It

is believed that the reflective mind is a good source of ideas, which may be used to formulate a good research

problem.

*** Folklores:**

Common beliefs could be right or wrong For example, it is generally believed that studying just before the test

decreases the score. We believe we should not study j before test to relax our mind. Researchers can conduct a

research study on whether one should study before the test or not.

***Exposure to field situations:**

During held exposure, researchers get variety of experience which may provide plenty of ideas to formulate research

problems. For example, whir working in field, a researcher observed a specific traditional practice for cure of a disen

condition, which can be used as research problem to investigate its efficacy.

*** Consultations with experts Experts** are believed to have sound experience of their spective field, which may suggest a significant problem to be studied In addition, expen may help in finding a current problem of discipline to be solved, which may serve as hass for formulation of research problem.

Q.15. Criteria For Selecting Research Problem?

= Criteria for Selecting a Good Research Problem

One commonly used acronym to define the criteria for a good research problem or question is FINER, where F stands

for **feasible**, I for interesting, N for **novel**, E. **for ethical**, and R **for relevant.** However, there are many factors that

should be considered while deciding credibil ity of a particular research question for a scientific investigation. Some of the most essential factors are discussed below:

-Significance to nursing profession: A problem that a researcher is selecting should have significance to nursing profession or it will not serve any purpose. A research problem is significant for nursing profession when it is directed to develop or refine the body of pro fessional knowledge. A research problem could be considered significant for nursing pro fession if it fulfils the following criteria:

Benefits nursing profession and patients, nurses, and health care fraternity through the study

• Improves clinical nursing practices through the results.

•Promotes nursing theory development or testing. Provides solutions of current nursing practice needs Generates information to get practical implications for nursing, profession

•**Original:** It is fundamentally considered that every research problem should be new and unique in itself. Therefore, it is the key responsibility of a researcher that an innovative knowledge is used for selecting a research problems, so

as to extend the growth of existing body of knowledge in a profession.

•**Feasible**: Feasibility is an essential consideration of any research project. Regardless of how significant or researchable a problem may be, the feasibility of research problem in reference to time, availability of subjects, facilities, equipment and money.and ethical considerations should be checked. It will help the researcher to decide whether selected problem is appropriate or inappropriate and study can becarried out or not.

Time: A nurse might be interested in studying sibling relationships among quintuplets Knowledge of the incidence of quintuplet births would certainly discourage anyone considering research on this particular population unless the researcher plans to make this a lifetime project. So, time is always a factor to be considered. It is wise to allow more time than seems to be needed because unexpected delays frequently occur.

• **Cost:** All research projects cost money, some studies are much more expensive than others. The researcher must consider realistically the financial resources available. Equipment and supplies: All research projects require some

type of resources. There fore, before making the final decision to conduct a study,an accurate determination of the needed equipment and supplies should be ensured. Some questions that should be answered before beginning a research project include:

What Is this is the equipment that will be needed? s equipment available and i in proper working order?

Is there a qualified operator of the equipment? Are the necessary supplies available or can they be obtained?

If the researcher takes into consideration equipment and supplies in the early phases of a research project, there are less chances of the project to be revised or discarded later because of equipment or supply problems.

• **Administrative support:** Many research projects require administrative support. The nurse researcher may find it very difficult to conduct research independently. Financial as well as psychological support from administration is

very helpful. Knowing that your superiors support your research efforts can be a very powerful motivating force.

Peer support: Many research ideas have never been developed because potential researchers received no support from their peers. One of the best ways to determine a researchable is through interactions and discussions with other nurses. A climate of shared interest in nursing research is essential among the members of the nursing

profession.

Availability of subjects: A researcher may believe that study subjects are readily available for the study. But this may not be the case. Potential subjects may not Solicit.

3. RESEARCH PROBLEM

meet the study criteria, may be unwilling to participate, or may already be partici pating in other studies. Therefore, availability of subjects must be ensured well in advance.

• **Researcher's competence:** A research problem can only be feasible if it is in accordance with researcher's competence, where researcher is capable to handle a given research problem.

Ethical considerations: A researcher must ensure that the research problem can be considered by the ethical

committee without undue hurdles. A very important topic of research cannot be considered feasible unit unless it is

in accordance with ethical guidelines.

• **Solvable/Researchable:** Problem selected is considered good only if it is solvable so that chances of insolvability of

problem should be minimized. Thus, it will enhance relevant results. For example, a researcher selects a research

problem to know the existence of God in this universe. These sorts of problems are ambiguous and impossible to solve. Therefore, the researcher must ensure that a research problem selected for the study is solvable.

• **Current:** A good research problem must be based on the current problems and needs of a profession, so that

results generated will be of more use. Furthermore, more number of the professionals will be interested in the

research conducted on the current issues of their profession.

Interesting: A research problem can only be considered good if it is in accordance with researcher's field of interest.

A research problem must be as per the motivation of the researcher and should be fascinating to the researcher, so that research is conducted with full enthusiasm and not merely for its accomplishment.

CHAPTER SIX

Hypothesis Assumptions

Q 1.Define Hypothesis

= The word hypothesis (plural is hypotheses) is derived from the Greek word 'hypotithenai' meaning 'to put under' or 'to suppose' for a hypothesis to be put forward as a scientific hypothesis, the scientific method requires that one can test it.

DEFINITION

According to Lundberg, "A hypothesis is a tentative generalization, the validity of which remains to be tested. In its most elementary stage, the hypothesis may be any hunch, guess, imaginative idea, which becomes the basis for action or investigation.

A hypothesis is a tentative assumption drawn from knowledge and theory which is used as a guide in the investigation of other facts and theories that are yet unknown.

Q 2. Types of Hypothesis

= **According to Lundberg,** "A hypothesis is a tentative generalization, the validity of which remains to be tested. In its most elementary stage, the hypothesis may be any hunch, guess, imaginative idea, which becomes the basis for action or investigation.

TYPES OF HYPOTHESES

Hypotheses are classified in several ways. With reference to their function.

Hypotheses are of two types:

(a) Descriptive hypotheses and

(b) Relational hypotheses.

Another approach is to classify them into: (c) Working hypotheses, (d) Null hypotheses and (e) Statistical hypotheses.

Third approach is to divide them on the basis of the level of abstraction. Three broad levels may be distinguished: (i) simple description, (ii) logical derivation, and (iii) abstraction.

Accordingly there are three types of hypotheses: (f) common-sense hypotheses, (g) complex hypotheses and (h) analytical hypotheses.

Descriptive hypotheses: There are propositions that describe the characteristics (such as size, form of distribution) of a variable. The variable may be an object, person, organisation, situation or event. Some examples are:

"Patient who attend pre-operative education classes less post-operative emotional stress than have patient who do not."

"The rate of unemployment among Nursing graduates is lesser than that of medical graduates."

Relational hypotheses: These are propositions, which describe the relationship between two variables. The relationship suggested may be positive or negative correlation or causal relationship. Some examples are:

"Families with higher incomes spend more for recreation."

"Upper-class people have fewer children than lower-class people."

"Labour productivity decreases as working duration increases."

Causal hypotheses :state that the existence of, or a change in, one variable causes or leads to an effect on another variable. The first variable is called the **independent variable**, and the latter the dependent variable. When dealing with causal relationships between variables the researcher must consider the direction in which such relationships flow, i.e. which is cause and which is effect **e.g., smoking causes lung cancer.**

Working hypotheses: While planning the study of a problem, hypotheses the formed. Initially they may not be very specific. In such cases, they are referred to as "Working Hypotheses" which are subject to modification as the investigation proceeds.

Null hypotheses: These are hypothetical statements denying what are explicitly indicated in working hypotheses. They do not, nor were ever intended to exist in reality. They state that no difference exists between the parameter and the statistic being compared to it. For example, even though there is relationship between a family's income and expenditure on recreation,

a null hypotheses may state: **"There is no relationship between families' income level and expenditure on recreation."** Null hypotheses are formulated for testing statistical significance, since, this form is a convenient approach to statistical analysis. As the test would nullify the null hypotheses, they are so called.

Statistical hypotheses: These are statements about a statistical population. These are derived from a sample. These are quantitative in nature in that they are numerically measurable, e.g., "Group A is older than Group B."

Common sense hypotheses: These represent the common sense ideas. They state the existence of empirical uniformities perceived through day to day observations. Many empirical uniformities may be observed in business establishments, the social background of workers, and the behaviour patterns of specific group like students e.g., "shop-assistants in small shops lack motivation." "Soldiers from upper class are less adjusted in the army than lower class men"; "fresh students conform to the conventions set up by seniors."

Complex hypotheses: These aim at testing the existence of logically derived relationships between empirical uniformities. For example, in the early stage Human ecology described empirical uniformities in the distribution of land values, industrial concentrations, types of business and other phenomena. Further study and logical analysis of these and other related findings led to the formulation of complex hypotheses such as "The concentric growth circles characterize a city," "Members of minority groups suffer from oppression psychosis," etc. Such hypotheses are purposeful distortions of empirical exactness.

Analytical Hypotheses: These are concerned with the relationship of analytic variables. These hypotheses occur at the highest level of abstraction. These specify relationship between changes in one property and changes in another. **For example, the study of human fertility might show empirical regularities by wealth, education, region, and religion. If these were raised to the level of ideal type formulation, one result might be the hypotheses: "There are two high-fertility population segments in India viz., low income urban Muslims and low-income rural low caste Hindus." At** a still higher level of abstraction, the effects of region, education and religion or fertility might be held constant. This would allow a better measurement of the relation between the variables of wealth and fertility.

Q. 3. Improtance of Hypothesis

= **According to Lundberg,** "A hypothesis is a tentative generalization, the validity of which remains to be tested. In its most elementary stage, the hypothesis may be any hunch, guess, imaginative idea, which becomes the basis for action or investigation

It is A researcher's eye,

- It focuses a research .
- It formulates clear and specific goals
- It links related facts
- It prevents blind research
- It works as a beacon light

1. Hypotheses facilitate the extension of knowledge in an area.

2. Hypotheses provide the researcher with rational statements,

3.Hypotheses provide direction to the research.

4. Hypotheses provide the basis for reporting the conclusions of the study.

5. Hypothesis has a very important place in research although it occupies a very small pace in the body of a thesis.

Q 4. ASSUMPTIONS

= Assumptions are things that are accepted as true, or at least plausible, by researchers and peers who will read your dissertation or thesis. In other words, any scholar reading your paper will assume that certain aspects of your study is true given your population, statistical test, research design, or other delimitations.

An assumption is a belief that forms one of the bases for the research. This belief is not to be tested or supported with empirical data. Very often belief is not stated in a research proposal.

Definition:

1. According to Charles An assumption is a proposition that is taken for granted, as if it were true based upon presupposition without preponderance of the facts.

2. According to Chris Jordan: An assumption is an accepted cause and effect relationships or estimates of the existence of a fact from the known existence of other fact (s).

3. According to Frederick: An assumption is an ascertain about some characteristic of the future that underlies the current operations or plans of an organization.

Need of assumptions: 1. This is important, because both assumptions and limitations affect the inferences you can draw from your study.

2. One of the more common assumptions made in survey research is the assumption of honesty and truthful responses.

3. However, for certain sensitive questions this assumption may be more difficult to accept, in which case it would be described as a limitation of the study

For example, asking people to report their criminal behaviour in a survey maynot be as reliable as asking people to report their eating habits.

Types of assumptions:

1. **Explicit assumptions**: Explicit assumptions are assumptions of which the intention that is fully revealed expressed without vagueness, implication or ambiguity.

2. Implicit assumption: Implicit assumptions are assumptions that are not expressed and may go undetected. If implicit assumptions prove to be wrong, this can damage projects.

ASSUMPTIONS

3. Primary assumption: Primary assumptions are assumptions about which the respondent identifies what they want, how dense the customer population is, what they need and what the customer sees as the alternative to your project, the primary assumptions define the foundation of an organization.

4. Derivative assumptions: Derivative assumptions come from the primary assumptions. The numbers in a sales forecast are based on assumptions about customerdemand, the number of clients; a sale person can visit in a week, the availability of the project.

Steps involved in assumption based planning:

1. Identify assumptions Collect all assumptions implicit, explicit, and primary and derivatives, out of the plan.

2. Determine criticality :Try to quantify the assumptions as much as possible in order to determine which assumptions have the greatest impact.

3. Design tests: Design a test foe every critical assumption.

4. Schedule test: Every critical assumption needs to be tested, but not all assumptions can be tested in the present, so future assumptions tests are scheduled in a test schedule, some possible reasons to schedule a test in the future are a lack of information in the present or dependency on the test outcomes of other tests.

5. Test assumptions: When an assumption is tested this results in a test outcome, which proves the assumption right or wrong. .

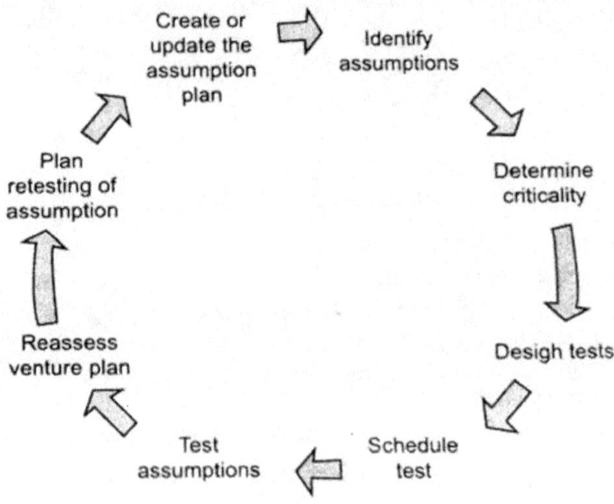

Flow Chart - 6.5 : Steps Involved in Assumption Planning

6. Reassess venture plan: Based on the test outcomes and the test schedule one might decide to reassess the venture plan and update theplan withthe new insights gathered into the assumption based planning process.

7. Plan retesting of assumption :The assumptions need to be re-tested regularly if not constantly. There should be a retest schedule of every critical assumption.

8. Create or update the assumption plan: The assumption plan holds all data gathered during the assumption planning process.

Q 5. Types of Error.

= In the contexts of testing hypothesis, there are two types of errors. They are type-l and type-ll error.

Type-l: we may reject H0, when HO is true and it is known as type-l error.

Type-ll: we may accept H0, when in fact HO is not true and it is known as type-ll error.

Types-1 error also known as alpha error and type-ll error also known as beta error.

Q 6. Characteristics of A Hypothesis

= CHARACTERISTICS OF A GOOD HYPOTHESIS

An acceptable hypothesis should fulfil conditions as given below:

1. Conceptual clarity: A hypothesis should be conceptually clear. It should consist of clearly defined and understandable concepts. Clarity is obtained by means of defining operationally the concepts in the hypothesis.

2. Specificity: A hypothesis should be specific and explain the expected relations between variables and the conditions under which these relations will hold e.g., "when there is dissatisfaction and no care is taken, deprivation will engender violence."

3. Testability: A hypothesis should be testable and should not be a moral judgement. It should be possible to collect empirical evidences to test the hypothesis. Statements like "Bad partners produce bad children" are common place generalizations and cannot be tested, as they merely express sentiments and their concepts are vague.

4. Availability of techniques: Hypotheses should be related to available techniques. Otherwise they will not be researchable; therefore, the researcher must make sure that methods are available for testing his proposed hypotheses.

5. Theoretical relevance: A hypothesis should be related to a body of theory. A science can be cumulative only by building on an existing body of facts and theory. It cannot develop if each study is an isolated investigation. When research is systematically based upon a body of existing theory, a genuine contribution to knowledge is more likely to result. Therefore, a hypothesis should possess theoretical relevance.

6. Consistency: Hypotheses should be logically consistent. Two or more propositions logically derived from the same theory must not mutually contradictory.

7. Objectivity: Scientific hypotheses should be free from value - judgement. In principle, the researcher's system of values has no place in scientific method. However, as social phenomena are affected by the milieu in which they take place, the researcher must be aware of his values and state them explicitly.

8. Simplicity: A hypothesis should be a simple one requiring fewer conditions or assumptions. But simple does not mean obvious. Simplicity demands insight. The more insight the researcher has into a problem, the simpler will be his hypothesis about it.

CHAPTER SEVEN

Review of Literature

Q 1. DEFINITION OF REVIEW OF LITERATURE

= The review of literature is defined as a broad, comprehensive in depth, systematic and critical review of scholarly publications, unpublished scholarly print materials, audiovisual material and personal communications.

According to Virginia Cano: review of literature to review a critical summary and an assessment of current state of knowledge or current state of the art in a particular field.

According to Chris Jordan: review of literature is the selection of available documents (both published and unpublished) on the topic, which contains information, ideas, data and evidence written from a particular standpoint to fulfill certain aims or to express certain views on the nature of the topic and how it is to be investigated, and the effective evaluation of these documents in relation to the research being proposed.

Q 2. PURPOSES OF LITERATURE REVIEW

= The review of literature is defined as a broad, comprehensive in depth, systematic and critical review of scholarly publications, unpublished scholarly print materials, audiovisual material and personal communications.

According to Virginia Cano: review of literature to review a critical summary and an assessment of current state of knowledge or current state of the art in a particular field.

Research is ongoing process that builds on previous knowledge. There are very few topics so rare that have never been investigated.

There are many purposes for reviewing the literature before conducting a research study.

1. Identification of a research problem and development or refinement of research question or hypothesis

2. To demonstrate familiarity with a body of knowledge and to establish credibility.

3. To show the path of prior research and how a current project is linked to it. 4.To integrate and summarize what is known in an area.

5. To learn from others and stimulate new ideas.

6. Orientation to what is known and not known about an area of inquiry, to ascertain what research can beast make a contribution to the existing base of evidence.

PURPOSES OF LITERATURE REVIEW

7. Determination of any gap or inconsistencies in a body of research.

8. Determination of a need to replicate a prior study in a different setting or with a different study population.

9. Identification or development of new or refined clinical interventions to test through empirical research.

10. Identification of relevant theoretical or conceptual for a research problem.

11. Identification of suitable designs and data collection methods for a study.

12. For those developing research proposals for funding, identification of experts in the field who could be used as consultants.

13. Assistance in interpreting study findings and in developing implications and recommendations.

Q 3. EXPLAIN SOURCES OF THE LITERATURE REVIEW

= The types of information sources for a review of literature are conceptual and data-based literature. The common sources of both these literatures are books, chapters of books, journal articles, abstracts, critique reviews, abstracts published in conference proceedings, professional and governmental reports, and unpublished doctoral dissertations and thesis. The kinds of information available in written documents can be categorized into five broad classes:

1. Facts, findings or results.

2. Theory.

3. Research procedure or methods.

4. Opinions, points of view or personal commentaries.

5. Anecdotes or impression on a particular event or situation.

The references can be categorized as being either primary or secondary sources.

Primary Sources

A primary source is written by a person. Who developed the theory or conducted the research or is the description of an investigation written by the person who conducted it. Most primary sources are found in published literature, e.g. nursing research article. A credible literature review reflects the use of mainly primary sources.

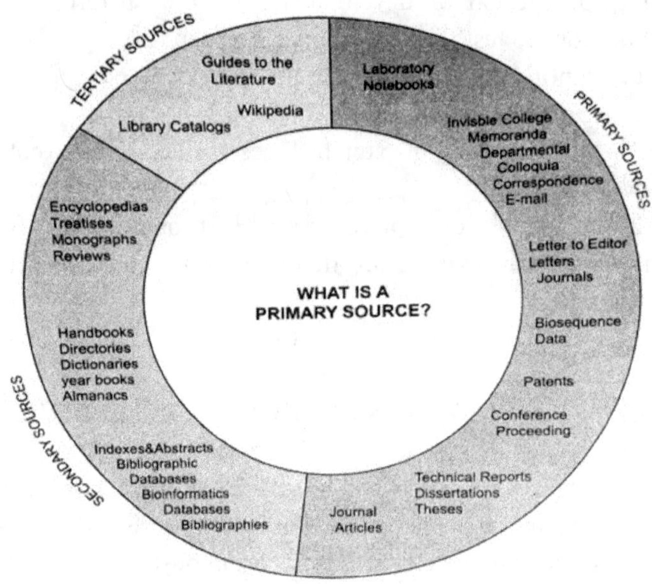

SOURCES OF THE LITERATURE REVIEW

Secondary Sources

A secondary source is written by a persons other than the individual who developed the theory or conducted research. Otherwise, known as it is description of study or studies prepared by someone other than the original researcher.

Often secondary source represents a response to, or a summary and critique of a theorist or researcher's work. The secondary sources may be used when unavailability of primary sources, and if we want to know different ways of looking at an issue or problem.

Q 4. Steps in Review of Literature

= The preliminary review generally includes three steps:

1. Identification of important publications-earlier works, reports, recent publications-Journals books MEDLARS, MEDLINC CAT-LINE.
2. Summarize and record the contents of publication contents-such as theoretical perspective, definitions, research design
3. Comparison of content such as theoretical perspectives, definations, research, design, methods, instruments, and findings

WAy to Review

1. To select a pertinent books or article from a general review of the literature, examine the book or article quickly. For a book, examine the title page that gives the author credentials then scan the table of contents, the index, the bibliography, and the charts and table. Reac the preface rapidly to determine the author's purpose; then thumb through the chapters quickly to assess substance. If the book is promising, keep it for a critical review. For article, examine the author's credentials, quickly scan the problem statement, and the hypotheses, and then focus on the methods of research used, especially how the sample was selected and the data analysed. Read conclusion and summaries and note the use of theory and other research studies. Retain sound and pertinent literature for summary and critique.

2. To summarise and record information, first note the author, title of the article, and year of publication. If further information is needed, this immediately refers to the reader to the bibliography card.

3. Record informations from a research report in the following order(s):

- Problem statement
- Definition of concepts
- Hypothesis if any
- Theories or assumptions used
- Method of research including how samples were drawn

- Instruments and scales used
- Type of research (description or explanation)
- Methods and findings of data analysis
- Interpretations of data especially whether hypothesis supported or rejected
- Recommendations and suggestions for further research if any
- Make special note of implications for nursing practice or theory.

4. Note that data was not included, such as limitations that were not noted, means of establishing the validity and reliability of instruments that was not given, theory that was not used, or former studies that were not examined.

Comparison of the recorded summaries of literature enables the researcher to contrast definitions of concepts, uncovered competing theories used to explain the same phenomenon, consider the various designs that have been utilized to study the same problem, examine different methods of data collection, and find valid instruments already developed.

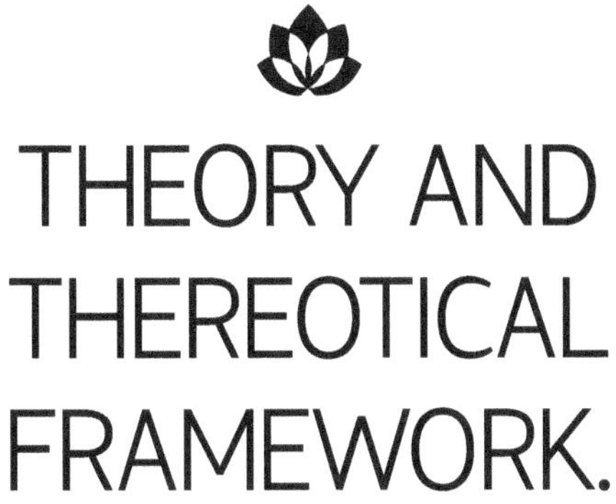

CHAPTER EIGHT

THEORY AND THEREOTICAL FRAMEWORK.

Q 1. Define Theory

= **DEFINITIONS OF THEORY**

"A theory" is a statement that purports to account for or characterise some phenomenon" and that it "Pulls out the salient parts of a phenomenon so that one can separate the critical and necessary factors or relationships from the accidental or unessential factors or relationship" (Barnum 1990).

"A theory is a set of concepts interrelated to form propositions that are useful for prediction and control."

"A theory is a conceptual system or framework invented for some purposes" (Dickoff and James 1968).

"A theory is a set of interrelated constructs (concepts adapted for a scientific purpose), definitions and propositions that present a systematic view of phenomena by specifying relations among variables, with the purpose of explaining and predicting the phenomena" (Kerlinger, 1986).

Q 2. Explain the Purposes of Theory

= Nursing theory serves many purposes. Among these purposes are:

1. To develop research propositions

2. To serve as a reservoir for knowledge and research findings

3. To explain observations and predict outcomes

4. To stimulate new directions in practice and in research.

Q 3. Discuss about the importance of nursing theories in formulation of conceptued frame work with any one example each.

= There are many theories which are reported in the nursing literature. For example, learning theory, developmental theory, theories of adaptation, stress and homeostasis theory, systems theory, social theories and cultural theories.

Learning theory includes theories of conditioning, social learning and cognitive theory.

Developmental theory examines changes that occur through time, in the physical, psychological and social structures.

Theories of adaptations, stress and homeostasis examine how individuals or groups survive and function in a particular environment.

System theory is diverse, focussing at times on behavioural systems and at other times on systems of interaction and communication or adaptation modes.

Social theories examine factors that are external to individuals, such as social class, but that affect their life chances and lifestyles.

Theories of symbolic interaction, such as Role Theory seek to explain how symbols and meanings establish the rules, roles, roles and images of self and others in daily life. C

ultural theories examine how traditional ways of life affect the behaviour, values, beliefs, and perceptions of individuals and groups.

The investigator uses theory in research to provide a framework constructed from past ideas, understanding, and research findings, and to provide foundations for the proposed research project, and he/she also uses theory to generate hypothesis.

Nursing theory is a source of professional autonomy and power. Theory provides nurses with a sound basis to describe explain, and predict factors that, influence nursing care.

The recurrent theme in nursing theory guides nursing education, research, and practice and differentiate nursing practice from other disciplines. In short, theory provides a firm basis for planning and considering our actions and for challenges nursing practice and theory itself.

Nursing theory enables nurses to predict outcomes of what they are doing and to explain their selection of patient care approaches.

Q 4. PURPOSE OF CONCEPTUAL FRAMEWORK

= 1. Its overall purpose is to make research findings meaningful and generalizable.

2. Frameworks are efficient mechanisms for drawing together and summarizing accumulated facts, sometimes from separate and isolated investigations.

3. Theories and model can guide the researcher's understanding of not only the "what" of natural phenomena but also the "why" of its occurrence.

4. Models help to stimulate research and the extension of knowledge by providing direction and important (drawing force).

Q 5. Difference Between Therotical and conceptual frame work.

=

Table - 8.1 : Difference Between Theoritical and Conceptual Framework	
Theoritical framework	**Conceptual framework**
A theoretical framework provides a broad explanation of relationships that exists between concepts	A conceptual framework is not as well developed as is a theoretical framework
A theoretical framework is based on ONE theory	When no existing theory fits the concepts that the researcher wishes to study, the researcher may construct a conceptual framework
The concepts of the study relate back to the theory.	Can be used to describe and begin to explain the relationships of the concepts
Theoretical frameworks start out as a conceptual framework and with much research; develop into a research-based theoretical framework	

Therotical and conceptual frame work.

Q 6. Enlist the stapes for development of a conceptual framework.

= framework of the study may be developed by using following steps

Identification of the general concepts: Initially, the researcher identifies the general concepts of the study; these concepts may be based on study variables, previous research findings,. existing theories nund models. Some concepts may be identified from a real-life observation or experience.

Gathering relevant information: Once the researcher identifies the concepts, the next step involves gathering the relevant information about the concepts from the relevant existing theories, previous research findings, etc. This information helps the researcher to understand the concepts more empirically to establish the relationship between concepts for development of framework. A framework is based on a specific theory or theoretical model; researcher must read about them from primary sources.

Gathering relevant information about conceptsenables the researcher to judge the amount of empirical support the theory has received and perhaps also the way the theory must be adapted in framework.

▶ **Formulation of general scheme of relevant concepts:** After learning in-depth about the concepts, the researcher starts establishing the general relationship between the different related and relevant concepts. This schematic relationship is established through brainstorming and logical reasoning. If a researcher has identified the problem statement and later develops a conceptual framework, it requires an iterative approach.

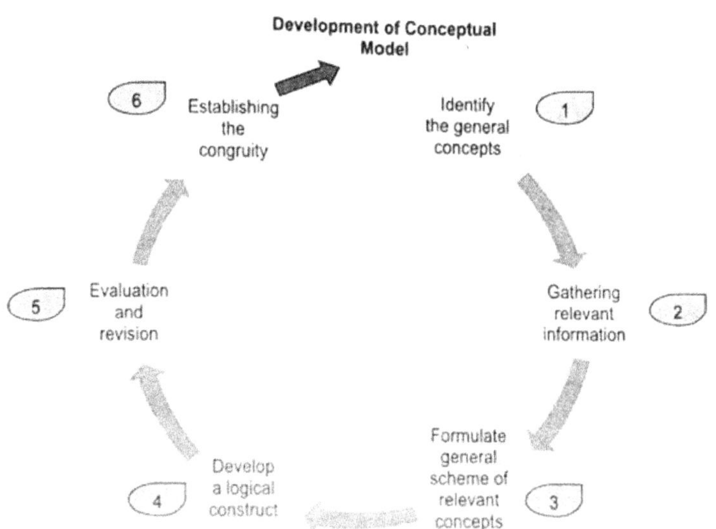

Stapes for development of a conceptual framework

▸ **Development of a logical construct:** After establishing the logical relationship between two more variables, the researcher develops a final construct. Construct is a highly abstract, complex description of a phenomenon (concept), and is denoted by a made-up or construed term. Construct term is used to indicate a phenomenon that cannot be directly observed but must be inferred by certain concrete or less abstract indicators of the phenomenon. For example, wellness, mental health, and self-esteem are constructs but they are only measured through indefinable and measurable concepts; for example, wellness can only be assessed with laboratory data.

▸ **Evaluation and revision:** Concepts and constructs act as the building blocks for the framework, which are later evaluated for their relevance and relationship to conclude or generalize the facts. After the evaluation, revisions may be made before development of a framework.

Establishment of the congruity: Once a researcher develops a framework, it is important to establish the congruity between conceptual model and its components, the research problem, hypothesis, the description of the operationalization of concepts, and the selection of research design. In the real sense, congruity of framework may only be established, if most of the research decisions and interpretations of the study findings are based on the framework.

CHAPTER NINE

Research Design.

Q 1. Definition research design

= Research design is a blue print for conducting the study that maximizes control over factors that could interfere with the validity of findings. The research design guides the researcher in planning and implementing the study in a way that is most likely to achieve the intended goal.

The control provided by the design increases the probability that the study results are accurate reflection on of reality. Skill in selecting and implementing research design is important to improving the quality of the study and thus the usefulness of findings.

DEFINITION

Research design is a blue print for conducting the study that maximizes control over factors that could interfere with the validity of the finding.

Q. 2. List the type of research design. Explain non experimental research desing in details ?

= **Quantitative Research Design -**

In Quantitative Research Design, a researcher examines the various variables while including numbers as well as statistics in a project to analyze its findings. The use of graphics, figures, pie charts is the main form of data collection

measurement and meta-analysis (it is information about the data by the data).

Qualitative Research Design -

This type of research is quite contrary to quantitative research design. It is explanatory in nature and always seeks answers to "What's" and "How's". It mainly focuses on why a specific theory exists and what would be the

respondent's answer to it. This allows a researcher to draw a conclusion with proper findings. Case studies are mainly used in Qualitative Research Design in order to understand various social complexities.

NONEXPERIMENTAL RESEARCH DESIGN

Nonexperimental research design is one of the broad categories of research designs in which the researcher observes the phenomena as they occur naturally and no external variables are introduced. It is a research design in

which neither the variables are deliberately manipulated nor is the setting controlled.

In nonexperimental research, researchers collect data without making changes or intro ducing treatments. Data obtained are analysed and the results may lead to the formation of hypothesis that can then be tested

experimentally. Within a quantitative framework, the ob servations are represented by numbers that can be

statistically analysed. Areas of research interest that have not been examined in depth may be best understood by

conducting a de scriptive study. Data in nonexperimental research are generally collected through the use of

questionnaires, interviews, observations, literature reviews, and critical-incident technique.

Need of Nonexperimental Design

Nonexperimental research design is frequently used by the nurse researchers. Some of the study situations where only nonexperimental designs can be used to conduct a study are as

follows: The studies in which the independent variables cannot be manipulated.

The studies in which it is unethical to manipulate the independent variable, ie, manipulation may cause physical or psychological harm to subjects. The studies or research situations where it is not practically possible to conduct

experiments.

• Descriptive - type studies that do not require any experimental approaches. most suitable to improve the understanding about the nonexperimental research designs.

o Descriptive design Univariant descriptive design

• Exploratory descriptive design . Comparative descriptive design . Correlational/Ex-post facto design

• Prospective design

Retrospective design Developmental research design

• Cross-sectional design Longitudinal design Epidemiological designs.

Case-control studies

• Cohort studies

• Survey research design

Q2. FACTORS AFFECTING RESEARCH DESGIN

= Factors Affecting Research Design:

When a researcher has formulated a research problem, he/she has to focus on developing a good design for solving the problem. A good design is one that minimizes bias and maximizes the reliability of the data. It also yields maximum information, gives minimum experimental error, and provides different aspects of a single problem. A research design depends on the purpose and nature of the research problem. Thus, one single design cannot be used to solve all types of research problem, i.e., a particular design is suitable for a particular problem.

A research design usually consists of the following factors:

1. Availability of scientific information

2. Availability of sufficient data

3. Time availability

5. Availability of the money

6. Manpower availability

7. Magnitude of the management problem

8. Degree of Top management's support

9. Ability, knowledge, skill, technical understanding and technical background of the Researcher

10. Controllable variables

11. Un-controllable variables

12. Internal variables

13. External variables.

Q 3. Explain the Experimental research design .

= EXPERIMENTAL RESEARCH DESIGNS

Experimentation is the most scientifically sophisticated research method.

It is defined as 'observation under controlled conditions' Experimental research differs from nonexperimental design in one important aspect. The researcher using an experimental design is an active agent rather than a passive observer.)

Experimental research designs are concerned with examination of the effect of independent variable on the dependent variable, where the independent variable is manipulated through treatment or intervention(s), and the effect of these interventions is observed on the dependent variable.

All the experimental researches have a common characteristic, that is, manipulation of independent variable, but a true experiment also consists of the principles of randomization and control. The application of control is difficult when studies are conducted in natural settings on human subjects. Therefore, in nursing, experimental research design is not feasible to use, and quasi-experimental, pre-experimental, or nonexperimental studies are more frequently conducted.

According to Riley, Experimental research design is a powerful design for testing hypotheses of causal relationship among variables. Ideally in the experimental design the investigator throw in a sharp relief of explanatory variables in which he is interested, controlling and manipulating the independent variable and observing its effect on the dependent variable and minimizing the effect of extraneous variables, which might confound his results. **Experimental research design is further classified in true** experimental designs, quasi-experimental designs, and pre-example research design.

Q 4. Elements of experimental designs

= TRUE EXPERIMENT RESEARCH DESIGN

The true experimental design are those in which the researcher has a great deal of control over the research situation only with the use of true experimental design can causality be interfered with any degree of confidence with these types of design, the researcher can have some confidence that the independent variables was the cause of the change in the dependent variable.

Criteria for true experimental research design:

1. Manipulation: the term manipulation means that the independent or experimental variable is controlled by the researcher. The researcher has control overthe type of experimental treatment that is administered and who will receive the intervention.

2. Control: the second criteria for the true experimental design are the use of a comparison or control group. A control group usually indicates a group in an experimental study that doesn't receive the intervention /treatment.

3. Randomization: the third criterion for true experimental studies is the random assignment of subjects to groups. Random assignment ensures that each subject has an equal chance of being selected into any of the groups in the experimental study.

Q 4. Give the characteristics of true research design.

= CHARACTERISTICS OF TRUE EXPERIMENTAL DESIGN

True experimental research designs are those where researchers have complete control over the extraneous variables and can predict confidently that the observed effect on the dependable variable is only due to the manipulation of the independent variable. A true experimental research design must essentially consist of the following three characteristics: manipulation, control, and randomization.

Manipulation:

1. Manipulation refers to conscious control of the independent variable by the researcher through treatment or intervention(s) to observe its effect on dependent variable.

2. It is a conscious act by the researcher, where he or she varies the independent variable and observes the effect that manipulates on has on the dependent variable of interest.

3. For example, a researcher is conducting a study on the efficacy of chlorhexidine mouthwash on the prevention of ventilator-associated pneumonia (VAP) among patients admitted in ICUs.

4. In this example, chlorhexidine mouthwash is the independent variable, which is manipulated by the researcher, and is used as an intervention for the experimental group, while the control group is kept deprived of it to observe its effect on the incidence of VAP.

Control:

1. Control is another essential element of true experimental design.

2. Control refers to the use of control group and controlling the effects of extraneous variables on the dependent variable in which researcher is interested.

3. The subjects in the control and experimental groups are similar in number and characteristics, but the subjects in the control group receive no experimental treatment or any intervention at all.

4. The experimental group receives the planned treatment or intervention, and a comparison is made with the control group to observe the effect of this treatment or intervention.

5. However, generally in health care and nursing research, it is not ethically feasible keep a control group deprived of interventions; however, existing conventional method of interventions may be compared with experimental interventions.

6. The control of the effects of extraneous variables on the dependent variables can be ensured by using several conventional measures, but none of them is very convenient to use. Some of these measures can, however, control extraneous variables, which

include:

a. Matching:

b. Counterbalancing

C. Homogeneity by statistical test

Randomization:

1. Randomization means that every subject has an equal chance of being assigned to experimental or control group.

2. This is also known as random assignment of subjects, which involves the placement of study subjects on a random basis.

3. Through random assignment of subject under experimental or control group, chances of systemic bias is eliminated.

4. Randomization is used in true experimental research designs to minimize the threat of internal validity of the study and to eliminate the effect of extraneous variables on dependent variables.

5. Through randomization, on an average the characteristics of the subjects in experimental and control group are similar; thus influence of extraneous variables on dependent variable is eliminated by dispersing the variability of the subject characteristics equally in both the groups.

Q 5.Discuss the Strength and Limitations (Advantages & Disadvantages) of Experimental research design.

= Advantages / Strength

Experimental research designs are considered the most powerful designs to establish the causal relationship between independent and dependent variables.

Where the purpose of research is explanation, causal relationship may be established among the variables by experimentation, especially in studies involving physical objects, where the variables are more easily controlled than in human studies.

In these studies, the controlled environment in which the study is conducted can yield a greater degree of purity in observation.

Conditions not found in a natural setting can be created in an experimental setting, where the independent variable is manipulated by investigator.

In the experimental approach, we can often create conditions in a short period of time that may take years to occur naturally. For example, in genetic studies we can breed strains in very small time, which would take a long time in nature to occur.

When the experiment is conducted in a laboratory, experimental unit, or other specialized research setting, it is removed from the pressure and problems of real-life situations and the researcher can pursue his or her studies in a more leisurely, careful, and concentrated way.

Disadvantages

Most of the times, the results of experimental research designs cannot be replicated in studies conducted on human beings due to ethical problems.

For certain research problems, because of the danger to physical and psychological health of the human subjects, it is not possible to conduct experiments on human beings.

Many of the human variables neither have valid measurable criteria nor instruments to measure them. For example, patient welfare or level of wellness cannot be measured on any scale or by any instrument. In these situations, if a refined experimental design is used, there may be a mismatch of research design and the variable-measuring instruments.

In experimental studies conducted in natural settings like hospitals or community, it is not possible to impose control over extraneous variables.

Experiments are often impractical when the effect of independent variable may require a lengthy period of time before it can emerge as a response on the criterion measures. This situation exists for many of the variables in nursing. One of the main drawbacks to conducting experiments on the effects of nursing care on acutely ill, hospitalized patients is that the patients are discharged from hospitals in such short periods of time that there is little opportunity to study the effects as they occur. Only by a difficult and costly procedure, these discharged patients can be followed in their homes to observe the experimental results.

However, it is not always possible because of several constraints.

Q 6. Steps in Experimental Design

= Major Steps in Experimental Design are as follow,

1. Delineate the population or universe to be studied (i.e., the set of subjects or objects that share a common observable characteristic).

2. Select a sample from the population by random sampling.

3. By random assignment, subdivide the sample into two sub-samples.

4. Specify one sub-sample, the experimental group and other the control group.

5. Before introducing the independent variable, observe and record all important characteristics of the two groups.

6. Introduce the independent variable into the experimental group but with holds it from the control group.

7. After introducing the independent variable, observe the dependent variable in both experimental and control group.

8. Compare the changes that occur in the experimental group with those that may have occurred in the experimental group with those that may have occurred in the control group.

9. Record the difference

10. Compare these values with statistically computed values that judge the significance of the difference, and indicate whether or not the observed differences could have occurred by chance.

Q 7.Types of Experimental Design

= The investigator planning an experiment has many experimental design option to choose. Experimental designs fall into three major categories which are:

a. True or classical experimental design.

b. Quasi-experimental design.

c. Pre-experimental design.

The most commonly used in nursing studies, are discussed as nomenclature used and definitions developed by Campbell and Stanley (1963) as follows.

True or classical experimental design: There are three major designs in the true experimental design, viz.

1. Pre-test and post-test control group design
2. Solomon Four-group design
3. After/Post-test-only experimental design.

Q 8. CHARACTERISTICS OF RESEARCH DESIGN

= CHARACTERISTICS OF RESEARCH DESIGN

Design research investigates the process of designing in all its many fields. It is thus related to Design methods in general or for particular disciplines. A primary interpretation of design research is that it is concerned with undertaking research into the design process. Secondary interpretations would refer to undertaking research within the process of design.

Characteristics of research design

1. Objectivity: The findings obtained by the research should be objective. It is possible by allowing more than one person to agree between the final scores/ conclusion of the research.

2. Reliability: If the similar research is carried out time and again in a similar setting it must give similar result. So the researcher must frame the research questions to make it reliable and provide similar outcomes.

3. Validity: Any measuring device can be said to be valid if it measures what it is expected to measure and nothing else. To make a research valid the questionnaire framed before research must be framed accordingly.

4. Generalization: The information collected from given sample must be utilized for providing a general application to the large group of which the sample is drawn.

Q 8. Types of the **Quantitative Research** design.

=

Broad categories	Types of research designs	Main features
I. Experimental research designs	1. *True experimental design* –Post-test-only control design –Pre-test–posttest control group design –Solomon four-group design –Factorial design –Randomized block design –Crossover design	Manipulation of independent variable, in the presence of control group, randomization
	2. *Quasi-experimental design* –Nonrandomized control group design –Time-series design	Manipulation of independent variable, but absence of either randomization or control group
	3. *Pre-experimental designs* –One-shot case design –One-group pretest–post-test design	Manipulation of independent variables, but limited control over extraneous variables, no randomization and control group
II. Nonexperimental research designs	1. *Descriptive design* –Univariant descriptive design –Exploratory descriptive design –Comparative descriptive design	Accurate description of characteristics of individual, situation, or group, and the frequency with which a certain phenomenon occurs in natural setting without imposing any control or manipulation
		Univariant descriptive: Studies undertaken to describe the frequency of occurrence of a phenomenon rather than to study relationship *Exploratory:* Investigating the phenomenon and its related factors about which very little is known *Comparative:* Comparing occurrences of a phenomenon in two or more groups

	2. *Correlational/Ex post facto design* –Prospective design –Retrospective design	Examining the relationship between two or more variables in a natural setting without manipulation or control (cause and effect relationship) *Prospective:* Examining relationship from cause to effect *Retrospective:* Examining relationship from effect to cause
	3. *Developmental research design* –Cross-sectional design –Longitudinal design	Examining the phenomenon in respect to the time *Cross-sectional:* Examining the phenomenon only at one point in time *Longitudinal:* Examining the phenomenon at more than one point in time
	4. *Epidemiological designs* –Case-control studies –Cohort studies	The investigation of the distribution and causes of diseases in a population is known as epidemiology
	5. *Survey research design*	Survey studies are investigation in which self-reported data are collected from sample with the purpose of describing population or some variables of interest
III. Other additional research designs	1. *Methodological studies*	Research conducted to develop, test, and evaluate the research instruments and methods
	2. *Meta-analysis*	Quantitatively combining and integrating the findings of the multiple research studies on particular topic
	3. *Secondary data analysis*	A research design in which the data collected in one research is reanalysed by another researcher, usually to test new hypotheses
	4. *Outcome research*	Outcome research involves the evaluation of care practices and systems in place. It is used in nursing to develop evidence-based practice and improve nursing actions
	5. *Evaluation studies*	It is research design which involves the judgement about success of a programmes, practices, procedures, or policies
	6. *Operational research*	Operational research involves the study of complex human organizations and services to develop new knowledge about institutions, programmes, use of facilities and personnel in order to improve working efficiency of an organization

Q 9. Difference / Comparison between the Qualitative and Quantitative Research.

=

Basis For Comparison	Qualitative Research	Quantitative Research
Meaning	Qualitative research is a method of inquiry that develops understanding on human and social sciences, to find the way people think and feel.	Quantitative research is a research method that is used to generate numerical data and hard facts, by employing statistical, logical and mathematical technique.
Nature	Holistic	Particularistic
Approach	Subjective	Objective
Research type	Exploratory	Conclusive
Reasoning	Inductive	Deductive
Sampling	Purposive	Random
Data	Verbal	Measurable
Inquiry	Process-oriented	Result-oriented
Hypothesis	Generated	Tested
Elements of analysis	Words, pictures and objects	Numerical data
Objective	To explore and discover ideas used in the ongoing processes.	To examine cause and effect relationship between variables.
Methods	Non-structured techniques like In-depth interviews, group discussions etc.	Structured techniques such as surveys, questionnaires and observations.
Result	Develops initial understanding	Recommends final course of action

Q 10 . Steps of quantitative research process.

=

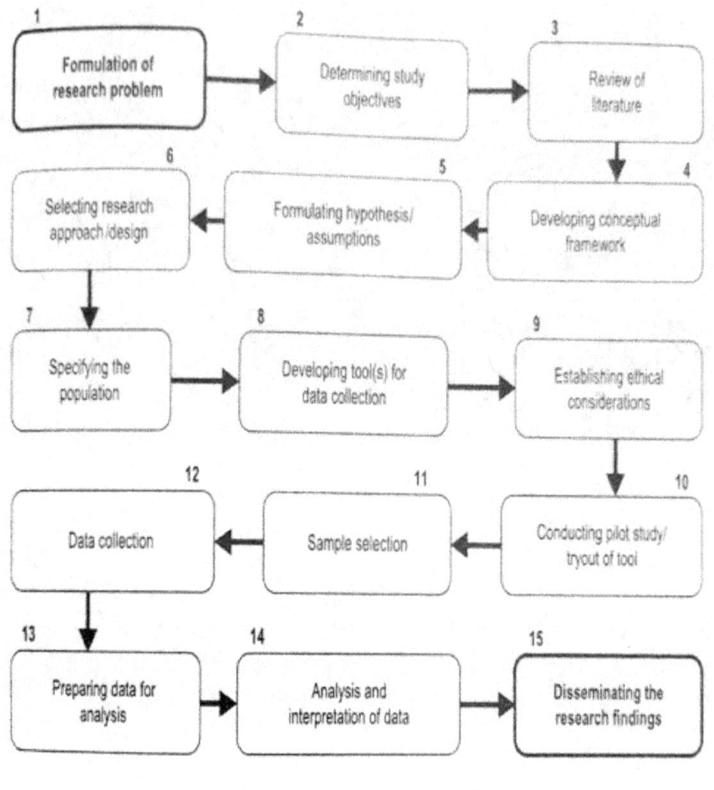

Steps of quantitative research process.

• Quantitative research is a formal, objective, and systemic process for generating information about the world. Quantitative research is conducted to describe new situation, events, or concept.

• The research process starts with the identification and formulation of research problem and end with the dissemination of research finding.

1. Formulation of research problem
2. Determining study objectives
3. Review of literature

4. Developing conceptual framework

5. Formulating hypothesis/assumptions

6. Selecting research approach /design

7. Specifying the population

8. Developing tool (s) for data collection

9. Establishing ethical consideration

10. Conducting pilot study/ tryout of tool

11. Sample selection

12. Data collection

13. Preparing data for analysis

14. Analysis and interpretation of data

15. Disseminating the research findings

1. Formulation of research problem

The foremost step of a research process is too discover an interesting and Research-worthy problem.

It is such an important step that the whole process can get wasted if the research problem is not clearly understood.

Therefore any good research need a good research problem.

The research problem must ensure features of originality, Solvability, and feasibility of research problem as well as

the need to take account it's following dimensions.

• Substantive dimension : is the research problem clinically or theoreticlly important?

• Methodological dimension: what is the best possible way to study his problem?

• Practice dimension: are adequate resources available to conduct the study?

• Ethical dimension: would this problem respect the right of the study subject?

2. Determining study objectives:

• There must be a clear direction to every research prom and objectives certainly serve this purpose.

• Therefore, researchers must have a lis objectives for the study, which provides the guidelines for the researcher as to w exactly must be done during the course of a particular research study.

• There may general and specific objectives for a research project.

• This step of the research process also includes writing operational definitions of variables under study. These

objectives and operational definitions not only help delimiting the research problem, but also provide a defined

direction to research proce where researchers have clarity about what to be studied under a particular statement

problem.

3. Review of literature:

• A literature review is a summary of previous knowledge generated the topic of study.

• It is believed by researchers that research cannot be conducted in a va uum, bereft of the previous

knowledge available, but that it requires a foundation of existi knowledge to plan and conduct a good research.

• This knowledge base can only be acquir through literature review from several sources, such as books,

journals, research repor unpublished theses, newspapers, magazines, and other current popular electronic inform

tion sources.

• Review of literature helps the researchers to understand what already known about a topic and what needs

to be further investigated. An effective litera ture review needs certain basic skills in researchers, such as critical

thinking, brainstorming reading, comprehending, analysis, synthesizing, and summarizing Literature review play an

important role in the development of research project and, moreover, researchers develop greater insight into the

research problem and gain information on what has been alread investigated regarding a particular topic under

study.

4. Developing conceptual framework:

• The basic aim of research in most disciplines is to develop, refine, or test theories.

• Nursing profession is considered as one of the oldest arts. but one among the youngest sciences, where

there is great need of developing new theories or refining/ testing existing theories to expand the body of

professional knowledge.

• Most of the nursing researchers plan to develop a conceptual framework based on the existing nursing or

other non-nursing theories. However, researchers may have their own concepts to develop new nursing-based

conceptual frameworks for research studies.

• These conceptual frameworks not only provide meaning to the research problem, but also help in

developing hypothesis or assumptions for the research studies.

5. Formulating hypothesis/assumptions:

• Hypothesis is an assumed statement suggesting an answer to a question, which may or may not be true.

• In simple words, it translates the statement of problem prediction of what is into a a clearly understandable

and easy-to-comprehend is expected to be the outcome of the study, which is either accepted or rejected based on

the empirical data generated at the end of the research process.

• For example, consider this research statement, 'A correlational study on alcohol intake and incidence of liver

disease among people of an urban community at Ludhiana' Here, hypothesis will be 'alcoholics have higher incidence

of liver disease".

• Assumptions are statements that are to be tested to be considered true, before they have been scientifically

tested. In other words, assumptions are the general beliefs of the people at large that are held to be true, but have

not necessarily been proven. For example, satisfaction is largely influenced by the preconceived expectations of the customers. This is a general belief of the people, but a researcher may use it as an assumption in a customer

satisfaction study. Generally, in nonexperimental research, investigators use assumptions or research questions to

have defined directions for the research study.

6. Selecting research approach/design:

• A research design is the systematic plan to obtain answers to research questions. In a broader sense,

research design is the blueprint of research study, which enables the researcher to know on whom, what, when,

whereand how the study will be conducted.

• Who: Specifies the subject(s) under study, eg. patients, families, groups, etc

• What: Specifies the variables that are to be focused upon and measured.

• When: Specifies the time of the study, duration, and frequency of the observations.

• Where: Specifies the setting of the study; that is where researcher will be conducting the study.

• How: Specifies how the data will be collected. For example, through manipulation of the variables in

experimental study under random assignment or simple questioning, inter view, or observation of a phenomenon

without manipulation and control over variables. Basically, there are three approaches/designs for the quantitative

research: experimental, quasiexperimental, and nonexperimental. However, these designs can be further

subclassified into several subtypes of each design.

• Experimental: In experimental researches, there is random assignment of subjects, and an availability of a

control group to compare with the experimental group, and manipulation of independent variable to observe effect

on dependent variable in an experimental group

• Quasiexperimental: Quasiexperimental studies involve manipulation of independent variables to observe effect on dependent variables, but usually they do not exert complete control over extraneous variables in

manipulation and randomization. Research studies on humans, in either field or clinical settings, make it impossible

to strictly imply the random assignment of subjects or control of manipulation and extraneous variables. Therefore,

health care professionals mainly conduct quasiexperimental research.

• Nonexperimental: In this design, research variables are studied without manipulating them in natural setting

for the purpose of description, exploration, explanation, or identification of correlation between two or more

variables.

7. Specifying the population:

• In quantitative research studies, it is essential to learn about the characteristics the subjects possess and

clearly define the group of subjects or objects under study. Research population is an aggregate of all the subjects or

objects with specific characteristics. For example, in study on 'prevalence of hospital-acquired infection among

patients admitted to intensive care units, population is patients admitted to intensive care units, where all the

patients are living in similar situation, Le. they are all admitted to intensive care units.

• Population specification helps the researcher to plan and develop an effective methodol ogy and tools sfor

the e development of empirical evidences

8. Developing tool(s) for data collection:

• This is the most important and crucial step of the t is essential to devise methods and tools to measure the

research vari research process It is ables as objectively and accurately as possible. The plan and design of the tools

for data collection depends on several factors, such as type of research design, variables, subjects, researcher's

expertise, available resources, and time for study.

• The researcher could use existing standardized research tools or may develop new tools, which must be

used after establishing their validity and reliability. In quantitative research, usually structured or semistructured

tools are used for data collection, which requires lot of constructive efforts, such as review of relevant content,

brainstorming, expert suggestions, and so on.

9. Establishing ethical considerations:

• In nursing science, most of the research is conducted on humans, where it becomes more important to

establish ethical consideration. During research studies, a researcher can address the ethical issues and may

establish ethical con siderations by taking the following measures:

• Taking informed consent from participants

• Avoiding errors in data collection.

• Obtaining the permission from competent authority to conduct the study.

• Doing justice to participants in analysing data.

• Maintaining confidentiality of the information and anonymity of subjects.

10. Conducting pilot study/tryout of tool: Pilot study is a kind of small-scalerehearsal on the subjects, but these

subjects are not a part of the actual study. Pilot study is conducted to ensure the feasibility of the study and revise

methodology and tool(s) of the study in caseof any shortcoming found.

11. Sample selection: It is not practically possible to conduct study on entire population. There fore, researchers

must select a representative part of the population. A sample can be selected by using either probability or

nonprobability sampling technique, where choice of sampling technique depends on several factors, like nature of

the study; availability of time, money, resources, and researchers' knowledge about population, etc. However, researchers always strive to select a representative sample which adequately reflects the population's trait.

12. Data collection: It is the most time-consuming step of the research process, which involves direct or indirect

interaction with respondents to gather information pertaining to the topic under study. It must be carefully planned

and implemented to collect relevant information by using preplanned methods, techniques, and tools of data

collection. Data collection requires adequate planning, patience, communication, interpersonal relationship, and

recording skills. Data could be collected through questioning, interviewing, or observation methods.

13. Preparing data for analysis: In quantitative studies, careful checking of every tool for its completeness and coding

is the main activity during this step of the research process. must be ensured that one code specifies only one piece

of information, and it should be maintained carefully to avoid any error. Coding can be carried out manually on a

paper sheet or on a computer grading sheet (eg. MS Excel sheet) or directly in statistical software.

14. Analysis and interpretation of data: In quantitative research studies, numerical data must be organized in an

orderly and sequential manner, and processing is required because research questions cannot be answered in

numerical form. In quantitative research, data may be analysed by using descriptive or inferential statistics.

Furthermore, data may be analysed either by manual calculations or by using statistical software programmes, like

Statistical Program for Social Sciences (SPSS). Data is presented through tables, graphs, and charts to facilitate the

interpretation of data.

15. Disseminating the research findings: Research may fail in achievement of its objectives, if findings are not

disseminated to its users. Research findings may be communicated through writing of research thesis, article, or presenting an oral research report at scientific professional conferences. Research finding must be communicated in

a standardized for mat according to the international, national, or institutional guidelines

Q 11. DEFINE EXPERIMENTAL RESEARCH DESIGNS & NONEXPERIMENTAL RESEARCH DESIGN

= Experimentation is the most scientifically sophisticated research method) **It is defined as 'observation under controlled conditions' Experimental research differs from nonexperimental design in one important aspect. The** researcher using an experimental design is an active agent rather than a passive observer.) Experimental research designs are concerned with examination of the effect of independent variable on the dependent variable, where the independent variable is manipulated through treatment or intervention(s), and the effect of these interventions is observed on the dependent variable. All the experimental researches have a common characteristic, that is, manipulation of independent variable, but a true experiment also consists of the principles of randomization and control.

NONEXPERIMENTAL RESEARCH DESIGN

Nonexperimental research design is one of the broad categories of research designs, in which the researcher observes the phenomena as they occur naturally, and no external variables are introduced. It is a research design in which variables are not deliberately manipulated, nor is the setting controlled.

Q. 12. Historical research design

=Introduction –

The systematic collection and criteria evaluation of data relating to past occurrence of particular phenomenon is also relies primarily quantitative data.Historical research is undertaken to answer questions

concerning causes , effects , or trends relating to past events that may shed light on present behavior or practices...

Characteristics of Historical research design

- It is important not to confuse Historical research with a review of literature about Historical events.

- Historical research involves the careful study and analysis of data about past events.

- Historical research is a critical investigation of events , Their development, experience of the past evidence.

- The purpose is to gain a clearer understanding of the impact of the past on present and future events related to the life process.It involves detailed analysis of what has been written.

- Is used to describe, explain, or interpret events.

- Generally ,Historical research involves the review of written materials but may include oral documentation as well.

- Historical research typically relies on available data.

- Historical method of research also covers categories such as Historical, legal,documentary, institutional,or organizational.

- Important existing data sources for nurse researchers are hospital records,nursing chart,physician order sheet,care plan statement.

Steps of Historical research

- First step : Data Collection

- Second step : Criticism of the data .

- Third Step : Presentation of the facts

\- ***First Step* :**

Comprehensive gathering of data is undertaken.historical sources of data usually classified two main categories that

is -

•Primary Sources - primary sources are First hand information that include –

1)oral or written records .

2)Remains or realic associated with person ,events,groups.

3) Documents classified as laws ,office records certificates, newspapers, magazines, maps,diagrams etc.

•Secondary source :

These are the reports of people who related the actual witness or actual participants in the same

For example- Most of the history books.

Second Step :Critism of the data.

The second step necessitate a comprehensive review of gathered materials.Two types of critism

1) External critism - The establishment of validity of the source.

2)Internal critism - the determination of reliability by correctly interpreting the contents of the document

Third Step : Presentation of the facts

After evaluating the Historical data ,the researcher must bring the material together to analyse it and to the

research hypotheses

Areas of Historical study

• Periods- Historical studies often focus on events and developments that occurred during particular blocks of time

in the past.

• Geographical locations- particular Geographical location e.g countries, cities

• Military history- is concentrates on the study of conflicts that have happened in human society.

Methods and tools used in Historical research

• Contemporaneous corroboration

• Photography

• Historical revisionism

• Change log

• Human evolution

• Social change .

CHAPTER TEN

Sampling

Q 1. ADVANTAGES AND DISADVANTAGES OF SAMPLING.

= **The advantages of sampling are as follows:**

Economy in expenditure:

If the data are collected for the entire population, cost will be very high. It is economical of cost, when the data are collected from a sample which is only a fraction of the population i.e., sampling helps to reduce the cost in the research.

Economy in time: The use of sampling is economical of time also. Sampling is less time consuming than census technique. Tabulation, analysis etc. also takes much less time in the case of a sample than in the case of a population. That means sampling helps greater speed in the project.

Greater scope: In many fields of enquiry (For example, quality control tests) where the complete destruction of the product is involved, a cent percent test production is impossible, and often, impracticable also, but they require highly trained personnel and sophisticated equipment. Sample simplifies things and personnel with little training can collect and handle data. There is a greater scope and flexibility of studies when a sample is used.

Greater accuracy: Sampling ensures completeness and a high degree of accuracy due to a limited area of operation. In dealing with a sample, the volume of work is reduced, therefore careful execution of fieldwork is possible. This processing of the data is also done more accurately, which in turn produces better results.

Organisation of convenience: Sampling involves very few organizational problems. Due to small numbers, it does not require vast facilities. It is economical in respect resources. The space and equipment required for this study are very small.

Intensive and exhaustive data: As the number is limited, it is possible to collect intensive and exhaustive data. Suitable in limited resources: In every society, there are more problems and less resources, particularly when the people are poor and problems uncountable. This is the method which enables the researcher to work even with limited resources.

Better rapport: It is very difficult to develop rapport of the large number of people, but it is possible to develop better rapport with the respondent / subjects.

Disadvantages of Sampling Chances of bias:

Sampling may involve biased selection and thereby lead to draw erroneous conclusions, may be due to various reasons.

Difficulty in getting representative supply: Selection of a truly representative sample is very difficult particularly when the phenomena under study are of a complex nature.

Need for specialised knowledge: In the absence of specialised knowledge, investigator may commit serious mistakes. So it requires specialised knowledge of sampling technique, statistical analysis and calculation of probable error.

Changeability of units: The cases of the sample may be widely dispersed, since many refuse to co-operate and some may be inaccessible and sometimes the selected cases may have to be replaced by others. All these introduce a change in the stipulated subjects to be studied.

Impossibility of sampling: Sometimes the universe is too small, or too heterogeneous, that, it is not possible to drive a representative sample. In such cases, supply is not required.

Q 2. Characteristics of a Good Sample

= 1. A good sample is one, which within restrictions imposed by its size, will reproduce the characteristics of the population with the greatest possible accuracy.

2. It should be free from error due to bias or due to deliberate selection of the unit of the sample.

3. It should be free from random sampling error.

4. There should not be any substitution of originally selected unit by some other more convenient in any way.

5. It should not suffer from incomplete coverage of the units selected for the study i.e., it should not ignore the failure in the sample in responding to the study.

6. Relatively small samples properly selected may be much more reliable than large samples poorly selected. But at the same time, it is very essential that the sample is adequate in size so that it can become more really reliable.

7. In the sample, only such units should be included, which as far as possible, are independent

8. While constructing a sample, it is important that measurable or known probability sample technique are used. This will substantially reduce the likely discrepancies.

Q . 3. Types of Sampling,.

= There are two main sampling methods for quantitative research: probability and non-probability sampling.

Probability sampling:

A theory of probability is used to filter individuals from a population and create samples in probability sampling. Participants of a sample are chosen random selection processes. Each member of the target audience has an equal opportunity to be a selected in the sample.

There are four main types of probability sampling

1. Simple random sampling: As the name indicates, simple random sampling is nothing but a random selection of elements for a sample. This sampling technique is implemented where the target population is considerably large.

2. Stratified random sampling: In the stratified random sampling method, a large population is divided into groups (strata) and members of a sample are chosen randomly from these strata. The various segregated strata should ideally not overlap one another. (Flow Chart)

3. Cluster sampling: cluster sampling is a probability sampling method using which the main segment is divided into clusters, usually using geographic and demographic segmentation parameters.

4. Systematic sampling: systematic sampling is a technique where the starting point of the sample is chosen randomly and all the other elements are chosen using a fixed interval. This interval is calculated by dividing population size by the target sample size.

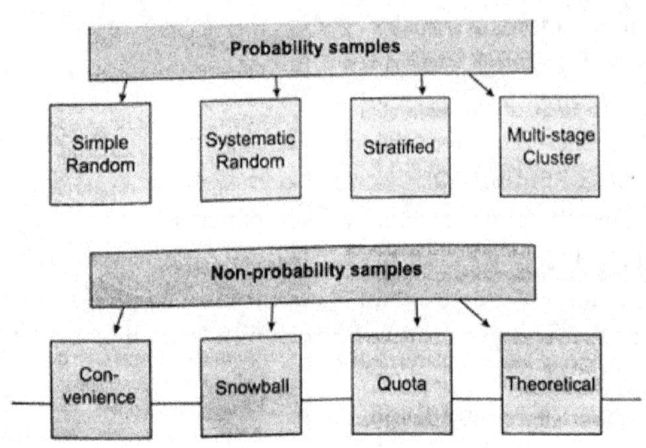

Types of Sampling

Non-probability sampling:

Non-probability sampling is where the researcher's knowledge and experience are used to create samples. Because of the involvement of the researcher, not all the members of a target population have an equal probability of being selected to be a part of a sample.

There are five non-probability sampling models:

1. Convenience Sampling: In convenience sampling, elements of a sample are chosen only due to one prime reason: their proximity to the researcher. These samples are quick and easy to implement as there is no other parameter of selection involved.

2. Consecutive Sampling: consecutive sampling is quite similar to convenience sampling, except for the fact that researchers can chose a single element or a group of samples and conduct research consecutively over a significant time period and then perform the same process with other samples.

3. Quota Sampling: Using quata sampling researchers can select elements using their knowledge of target traits and personalities to form strata. Members of various strata can then be chosen to be a part of the sample as per the researcher's understanding. Snowball Sampling ·

4. Snowball Sampling: snowball sampling is conducted with target audiences which are difficult to contact and get information. It is popular in cases where the target audience for research is rare to put together.

5. Judgmental Sampling: judgmental sampling is a non-probability sampling method where samples are created only on the basis of the researcher's experience and skill.

Q 4. Explain the Simple random sampling

= It is a probability sampling procedure in which the required number of sampling units are selected at random from the population in such a manner that each population element has an equal chance (probability) of being selected for the sample.

Each choice of a sampling unit must be independent of all other choices. One of the most acceptable methods for selecting a simple random sample is to use a table of random numbers, which can be either computer-generated or found in a statistics textbook. The numbers in a random-number table have been generated in such a way that there is no pattern. The same probability exists that any digit will follow any other digit, and each selection is an independent choice. To obtain a simple random sample, first list each of the population elements, then assign consecutive numbers to each of these elements. Then, referring to table of random numbers, arbitrarily start at any point in the table and proceed in any direction to identify enough tabled numbers to associate with the population elements until the desired sample has been selected.

Merits

1. This method requires minimum knowledge about the population in advance which is needed in the case of purposive sampling

2. The method is free from classification errors

3. Sampling errors can be easily computed and the accuracy of the estimate easily assessed.

Demerits

1. This method does not make use of the knowledge about the population which researcher may have.

2. The size of the sample required to ensure statistical reliability is usually large under stratified sampling.

3. From the point of view of field survey, it has been claimed that cases selected by random sampling tend to be too widely dispersed geographically and that the time and cost of collecting data becomes too large.

4. The use of simple random sampling necessitates a completely catalogued universe from which to draw the sample.

But it is often difficult for the investigator to have up-to-date lists of all the elements of the population to be sampled.

Q 5. Explain the Stratified Random Sampling

= This is an improved type of random or probability sampling. In this method, the population is sub-divided into homogeneous groups or strata, and from each stratum, random sample is drawn.

For example, university students may be dividend on the basis of discipline, and each discipline group may again be divided into juniors and seniors; and the employees of a business undertaking may be divided into managers and non managers and each of those two groups may be sub-divided into salary-grade-wise strata.

Stratification is necessary for

(1) increasing a sample's statistical efficiency,

(2) providing adequate data for analyzing the various sub-populations, and

(3) applying different methods to different strata.

Stratification ensures representation to all relevant sub-groups of the population. It is thus more efficient statistically than simple random sampling.

Stratification is essential when the researcher wants to study the characteristics of population sub-groups, e.g., male and female employees of an organisation.

Stratification is also useful when different methods of data collection, etc. are used for different parts of the population e.g., interviewing for workers and self-administered questionnaire for executives.

Q 6. Explain Snowball Sampling

= It is also known as nominated sampling, is a non-probability sampling procedure study subjects are asked to provide referrals to other study subjects.

In this method of sampling, investigators identify individual respondents whom they believe to have pertinent information related to their study. They then ask these individuals to name (nominate) others who might be able to provide further information; these respondents, in turn, are then asked to name other potential respondents.

This sampling technique is also **termed network sampling or link-tracing sampling.**

This is the colourful name for a technique of building up a list or a sample of a special population by using an initial set of its members as informants.

For example, if a researcher wants to study the problem faced by Indians through some source like Indian Embassy. Then he can ask each one of them to supply names of other Indians known to them, and continue this procedure until he gets an exhaustive list from which he can draw a sample or make a census survey.

This sampling technique may also be used in socio-metric studies. For example, the members of a social group may be asked to name the persons with whom they have social contacts, each one of the persons so named may also be asked to do so, and so on. The researcher may thus get a constellation of associates and analyse it.

Advantages

• It is very useful in studying social groups, informal group in a formal organization, and diffusion of information among professionals of various kinds

. • It is useful for smaller populations for which no frames are readily available.

Disadvantages

• It does not allow the use of probability statistical methods. Elements included are dependent on the subjective choice of the original selected respondents.

• It is difficult to apply this method when the population is large.

• It does not ensure the inclusion of all elements in the list.

Q 7. Define Sampling and Explain probability sampling atifie random sampling techniques.

= **Defination:**

Sampling is a process of selecting representative units from an entire population.

Probability Sampling

Introduction :

It is one of a technique of sampling ,it is based on theory of probability.

It involves random selection of the elements from the population

Techniques of probability sampling :

1.Simple random sampling

2.Stratified random sampling

3.Systemic random sampling

4.Cluster/multistage sampling

5.Sequential sampling

I. Simple Random Sampling:

In this every member of population has an equal chance to getting selected. In this for the sampling used random

sampling technique. Due to the random selection there is a absence of systemic bias. Random selection either by a lottery, random table or computer.

ADVANTAGES :

Most realiable and unbiased method

Requires minimum knowledge of study population

Free from sampling errors

DISADVANTAGES:

Need up to date complte list of of all members of the population

Expensivre and time consuming

II. Stratified Random Sampling:

Dividing heterogeneous population in strata based on selected traits such as age , gender ,habitat ,and then

random selection of sample from each strata.

ADVANTAGES

Ensures representative sample in heterogeneous population.

Comparision is possible in two group.

DISADVANTAGES

Requires complete information of population

Large population is required

Chances of faulty classification of strata

III. Systematic Random Sampling:

Selecting of every Kth case from the group ,,such as every 10th person on a patient list or 100th person

ADVANTAGES:

Convenient and simple to carry out

Distribution sample over entire population

DISADVATAGES

Less representative sample if subjects are non randomly distributed

Sometimes may result in biased sample

IV. Cluster Or Multistage Sampling:

In very large population random selection of geographic cluster and then random selection of subjects from the

cluster. When population is very large such as "Asia" random selection of geographic cluster

ADVANTAGES:

Cheap, quick and easy for large population

Population parameters of population can be estimated for sample size

DISADVANTAGES:

Possibility of high sampling error

Chances of least presentative sample due to over represented or under represented cluster

V. Sequential Sampling:

The investigator initially select small sample and tries to make inferences ;if not able to draw result ,he/she then add

subjects until clear cut inferences can be drawn. Sample size is not fix continue till inference are drawn

ADVANTAGES

Study on best possible smallest sample

Facilitates inferences of study

DISADVANTAGES:

Not possible to study a phenomena which need to be studied to one point of time

Requires are repeated entry into field to collect the sample

CHAPTER ELEVEN

Research tool & Methods

Q 1. . Research tool

= DEFINITION

1. Research tool may be defined as: Anything that becomes a means of collecting information for your study is called a research tool or a research instrument. For example, observation forms, interview schedules, questionnaires, and interview guides are all classified as research tools.

2. Measurements are the process of assigning numbers to variables. Measurements, as used in research, imply the qualification of information that is the assigning of some type of numbers to the data.

MEANING OF TOOLS & METHODS

There are many alternatives to choose from when selecting a data-collection method. These methods include questionnaires, interviews, physiological measures, attitude scales, psychological tests and observational measures.

Q 2. Enumerate the Principals For research tool creation.

=

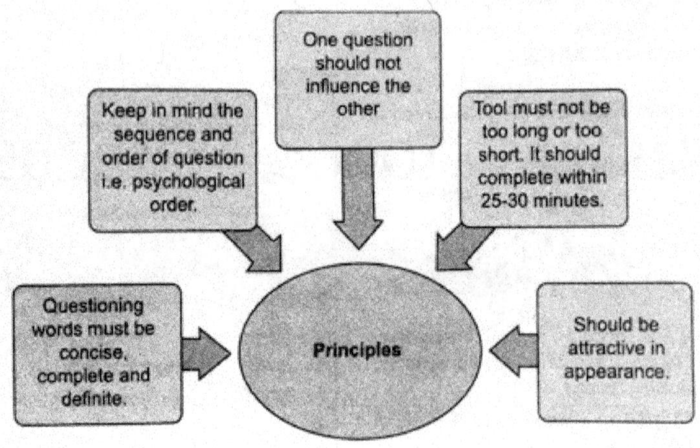

Principals For research tool creation.

Q 3. Define reliability of measuring Instrument .
=Definition:

1. According to **Chris Jordan,** Reliability is the consistency of a set of measurements or measuring instrument often used to describe a test.
2. According to **Houghton,** Reliability is an attribute of any system that consistently produces the same results, preferably meeting or exceeding its specifications.
3. . According to **Livingstone,** reliability is the ability of an item to perform a required function under stated conditions for a specified period of time.

Q 4. What are the factors affecting the reliability.
= 1. **Admistrative factors :**
Poor or unclear directions given during administration or inaccurate scoring can affect reliability.

For example: it says you were told that your scores on being social determined your promotion.

1. **Number of items on the instrument :**

The larger the number of items, the greater the chance of high reliability. For example, it makes sense when you ponder that 20 questions on your leadership style is more likely to get a consistent result than four questions.

1. **The instrument taker :**

The response portrayed by the individual respondent will vary with considerable stress and much interference is faced by him during the test. For example, if you took an instrument in august when you had a terrible flu and then in December when you were feeling quite good we might see a difference in your response consistency. If you were under considerable stress of some sort of if you were interpreted, while answering the instrument questions, you might give different responses.

4. Heterogeneity of the

The greater the heterogeneity (differences in the kind of questions of difficulty of the questions) of the times, the greater the chance of high reliability correlation coefficients. For example: if you throw a variety of questions, which is difficult to give an answer and also from various areas. Length of time between test and retest frame

5. Heterogeneity of the group members

The greater the heterogeneity of the group members in the preferences, skills or behaviors being tested, the greater the chance for high reliability correlation coefficients. For example, if the participants are from various professions the view will be different from one another.

6. length of time between test and reset.

The shorter the time, the greater the chance for high reliability correlation co-efficients. As we have experiences, we tend to adjust our views a little from time to time. Therefore, the time interval between experience intervals. Experience happens and it influences how we see things. Because internal consistency has no time lapse, one can expect it to have the highest reliability correlation co-efficient. For example, when less time is given between the test and retest regarding a particular topic the reliability will be High.

Outside factors that affect reliability

1. Fatigue, illness, emotions, motivational level, attitudes, and values, all affect reliability.

2. Motivation is probably a more important factor, especially the motivation to study before taking the test.

3. A student's personality characteristics may affect his or her test scores. Sociable persons who enjoy communicating, who are able to express themselves fluently will also often score higher than persons who lack such characteristics.

4. Students' past experience with tests will influence their performance on subsequent tests.

5. The quality of students' past experiences with tests, if they have often achieved success.

6. Students memory, fluency, and the like also enter into the reliability of a test. The higher these factors, the more reliable the test.

7. Lapses inattention, boredom, distractions, poor ventilation, and the like may serve to reduce a test's reliability to some extent.

8. In most cases, a teacher can increase reliability simply by ensuring that all students clearly understand test directions, are marking answer sheets correctly, and are not interrupted during the testing process.

9. Elimination of distractions and maxim insertion of students' comfort through good lighting, ventilation, and heating can also contribute to higher reliability.

Q 4. Types of reliability

= Test-retest reliability or stability

1. It refers to degree to which research participants response change overtime.

2. Test-retest method is used to test stability of the tool.

In this method an instrument is given to the same individuals on two occasions within relatively short duration of time

3. A correlation coefficient is calculated to determine how closely the participants' responses on the second occasion matched their responses on the first occasion.

Half-split reliability or internal consistency

1. It is a measure of reliability that is frequently used with scales designed to assess psychosocial characteristics.

2. Instruments can be assessed for internal consistency using half- split half technique (i.e. answers to one halfof the items are compared with answers to the other half of the items) or by calculating the alpha coefficient or using Kuder-Richardson formula.

3. In the case alpha coefficient and Kuder-Richarcison formula, a coefficient that ranges from 0 to 1.00 usually results.

Inter-rater reliability equivalence or the notion of equivalece

1. It is often concern when different observers are using the same instrument to collect data at the same time.

2. A coefficient can be calculated or other statistical or nonstatistical procedure can be used to see the correlation of values.

Q 5. Describe the methods for aseessing the reliability of mearing instruments.

= Methods of determining reliability

1. The most common method of determining an examination's reliability is the **test-retest method.**

Kuder Richardson Approaches

2. As explained previously, the same test is given to the same group on two separate occasions, usually a few days apart.

3. The correlation between the two tests becomes **the coefficient of reliability.**

4. Since rankings rather than raw scores are used to compute the correlation, the fact that most students usually do slightly better on the second test will not greatly affect final results.

5. The real problem with this method stems from students looking up answers after the first test.

6. Some students may not look up any answers, while others may look up as many as they can remember.

7. This would reflect intervening learning and would cause their scores to rise disproportionately. likely students talk about

8. The same problem may occur when the test among themselves. We could expect that those who discuss the test would improve their scores, whereas those who do not discuss it will not improve or will improve only slightly.

9. Another way to determine reliability is split-half correlation. Each student's test is divided in half, usually with odd-numbered items making up one-half and even-numbered items making up the other half. This produces two tests for each student that is then correlated with each other.

10. **A third method is to correlate some students'** scores on equivalent forms or two tests that cover the same material although the specific questions are different.

11. For example, the first test might contain the math problem 47 x 93, while the second contains 93 x 47.

12. It is impossible to develop two tests with different questions that are exactly equal in difficulty, but we can make them fairly close.

13. These two tests are then administered within a fairly short time period and, as before the results are correlated.

14. The problem with this method is that it costs time and money, and it is hard to ensure that the two tests are equal but different.

Q 6. How the Researcher can increase reliability.

= The various methods of determining reliability can never yield precise measures of a test's unreliability. Correlation coefficients are only estimates or, more precisely, averages. For a teacher, the most important concern is how to increase reliability. The following causes of unreliability should be avoided:

1. The sample of test items is skewed: That is, some material only briefly mentioned in class is made an important part of the test, while other material extensively covered in class is only briefly touched on. If a test is not well balanced and does not test material in proportion to the emphasis it was given in class or in the text, reliability will be lowered. To remedy this situation, a table of specifications should be used to balance the test.

2. Wording of instructions and questions is ambiguous. This common problem may cause students to misinterpret the intent of a question or a portion of the test. Ambiguity may be reduced by revising test questions in accordance with feedback 3 from other teachers or based on the results of previous use, either in a practice test or with other classes.

3. Too many difficult items can lead students to do a great deal of guessing. Chance then plays an important role in final scores. The more difficult a test is, the more its final scores are affected by chance. To solve this problem, the test should be made easier. The average difficulty level for a non-mastery test should be about 0.50.

4 . A short test usually has lower reliability. Probably the easiest way to increase a test's reliability is by lengthening it. An average test that contains only 10 questions often has very little reliability, whereas a test of 70 questions of equal quality is likely to have greater reliability. The Larger the sample, all other things being equal, the more accurate the assessment of student's level of achievement usually is.

3. Restrictive time limits can force hasty reading and responding, which affect students' final scores. Students should generally be given plenty of time to finish a test. This ensures that they answer thoughtfully and minimizes quick guesses.

Q 7. Describe the pilot study in terms of the definition and importance.

= Meaning:

1. It is a small preliminary investigation of the same general character as the major study which is designed to acquaint the researcher with problems that can be corrected in proportion for the larger research project or is done to provide the researcher with an opportunity to try out the procedures for collecting data.

2. The pilot study then is miniature trial run of the methodology planned for the major project.

3. It is a time for detecting errors and flaws being made in the instrument for gathering data. Then when the actual study is carried out the researcher can profit by the mistakes made in the pilot study.

Definition:

1. According to Julie Stachowiak, A pilot study is a smaller version of a larger study that is conducted to prepare for that study.

2. According to short and Pigeon, Pilot studies are small-> scale rehearsals of larger data collections.

3. According to Gordon Marshall, A Pilot study is any small-scale test of a research instrument (such as a questionnaire experiment or interview-schedule), run in advance of the main fieldwork and used to test the utility of the research design.

IMPORTANCE

1. It tells us about the completeness, accuracy and convenience of sampling frame from which it is proposed to select the sample.

2. It unfolds the variability within the population to be surveyed. It is important for determining the sample size.

3. It helps in bringing out the inadequacies of the draft questionnaire.

4. Throws light on several difficulties in the study.

5. Shows the effectiveness of the training of the personnel or collecting data.

6. Allays interviewer's fear about overtly sensitive questions and builds their self-confidence.

7. Tests interviewer's stamina to work under conditions of personal discomfort, stress and fatigue.

8. Tests the efficiency of the survey organization in the field.

9. Helps in identifying the needs for different kinds of equipment, vehicles necessary during the project.

10. Provides data for making estimates of time and costs for completing various phases of the project and shows ways to effect savings.

11. Scale of pilot study will depend on the availability of resources like time, money and personnel.

12. Provides for initial analysis of the adequacy of the questionnaire and the training instructions and supervision under field conditions.

13. Aids to identify parts of the instrument package that are difficult for pretest subjects.

14. Helps to identify objectionable or offensive questions. 15. Assesses the sequencing of instrument to be sensible. 16. Determines the needs for training of data collection staff.

17. Determines whether the measurement yields data with sufficient variability.

Q 8. Define validity & Types of validity .

=Validity of an instrument refers to the degree to which an instrument measures what it is supposed to be measuring. For example, a temperature-measuring instrument is supposed to measure only the temperature; it cannot be considered a valid instrument if it measures an attribute other than temperature. Similarly, if a researcher developed a tool to measure the pain, and if it also includes the items to measure anxiety, it cannot be considered a valid tool. Therefore, a valid tool should only measure what it supposed to be measuring.

Definitions

According to Treece and Treece, 'Validity refers to an instrument or test actually testing what it suppose to be testing'.

According to Polit and Hungler, 'Validity refers to the degree to which an instrument measures what it suppose to measuring'.

According to American Psychological Foundation, 'Validity is the appropriateness, meaning, fullness and usefulness of the interference made from the scoring of the instrument'.

Validity is the appropriateness, completeness and usefulness of an attribute measuring research instrument.

Types of Validity

Basically validity is classified into following four categories:

Face validity:

Face validity involves an overall look of an instrument regarding its appropriateness to measure a particular attribute or phenomenon. Though face validity is not considered a very important and essential type of validity for an instrument. However, it may be taken in consideration while assessing for other aspects of validity of a research instrument. In simple words, this aspect of validity refers to the face value or the outlook of an instrument. For example, a Likert scale designed to measure the attitude of the nurses towards the patients admitted with HIV/AIDS; a researcher may judge the face value of the this instrument by its appearance, that is it looks good or not; but it provides no guarantee about the appropriateness and completeness of a research instrument with regards to its content, construct, and measurement score.

Content validity: It is concerned with scope of coverage of the content area to be measured. More often it is applied in tests of knowledge measurement. It is mostly used in measuring complex psychological tests of a person. It is a case of expert judgment about the content area included in the research instrument to measure a particular phenomenon. Judgement of the content viability may be subjective and are based on previous researchers and experts opinion about the adequacy, appropriateness, and completeness of the content of instrument. Generally this viability is ensured through the judgments of experts about the content.

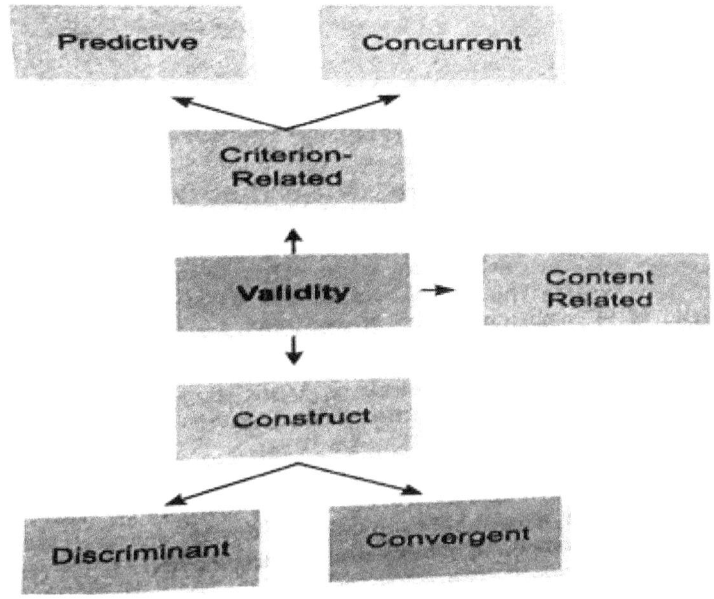

Types of validity

Criterion validity: This type of validity is a relationship between measurements of the instrument with some other external criteria. For example, a tool is developed to measure the professionalism among nurses; to assess the criterion validity nurses were separately asked about the number of research papers they published and number of professional conferences they have attended. Later a correlation coefficient is calculated to assess the criterion validity. This tool is considered strong with criterion validity if a positive correlation exists between score of the tool measuring professionalism and the number of research articles published and professional conferences attended by the nurses.

The instrument is valid if its measurements strongly respond to the score of some other valid criteria. The problem with criterion-related validity is finding a reliable and valid external criterion.

Mostly we are to rely on a less than perfect criterion because the rating found by empirical and supervisory methods may be computed mathematically, which can correlate score of instrument with scores of criterion variable. Here the range of coefficient >70 is desirable. Criterion-related validity may be differentiated by predictive and concurrent validity.

Predictive validity: It is the degree of forecasting judgement; for example some personality tests on academic futures of students can be predictive of behaviour patterns. It is the differentiation between performances on some future criterion and instruments ability. An instrument may have predictive validity when its score significantly correlates with some future criteria.

Concurrent validity: It is the degree of the measures in present. It relates to the present specific behaviour and characteristics; hence the difference between predictive and concurrent validity refers to timing pattern of obtaining measurements of a criterion.

Construct validity:

A construct is founded in this type of validity, such as a nurse may have designed an instrument to measure the concept of pain in amputated patients. The pain pattern may be due to anxiety; hence the results may be misleading. Construct validity is a key criterion for assessing the quality of a study, and construct validity has most often been addressed in terms of measurement issues. The key construct validity questions with regard to measurements are: What is this instrument really measuring? Does it adequately measure the abstract concept of interest? Construct validity gives more importance to testing relationship predicted on theoretical measurements. The researcher can make prediction in relation to other such type of constructs. One method of construct validation is known group techniqueAdd Chapter

CHAPTER TWELVE

Tools and method of Data Collection.

Q 0. Define Data Collection. List The Sources Of Data Collection. Explain Any One Method Of Data Collection In Detail.

= Definition:

"Data are the observable and measurable facts that provide information about the phenomenon under study.

In research studies, two types of data are collected; those are primary and secondary data."

"data is any information that has been collected, observed, generated or created to validate original research

findings. Although usually digital, research data also includes non-digital formats such as laboratory notebooks and diaries."

The sources of data collection are generally categorized in two broad categories, they are as following:

1.Primary sources

2.Secondary sources

1.primary sources:

Primary data are directly collected from the research units, which may be individuals, objects, programmes,

or institutions. Primary sources provide the first hand information collected by the researcher directly from the

respondents or the situa tions, which may be collected through interviews, questioning, observation, biochemical

measurements, and psychosocial measurement scale.

2.Secondary sources:

Secondary data are collected from either internal or external secondary sources. External sources involve existing materials, such as published or unpublished records. Published records may include the journals, magazines, newspapers, government reports, statistical abstracts, census reports, constituents of mass communication, and commission reports. Unpublished records may include official records, patient records, thesis, dissertations, and reports. In addition, internal secondary sources also known as private documents-may include the biographies, personal diaries, letters, memoires, etc.

The methods of data collection are as following:

1.Interview

2.Questioning

3.Observation

4.Biophysiologic methods

5.other methods

1.INTERVIEW:

Introduction:

The interview is a process of communication or interaction in which the subjects or interview gives the needed information verbally in a face-to-face situation.

Interviewing requires face-to-face contact or contact over telephone and calls for inter viewing skills. Interview may be used either as a main method or as a supplementary one in collection of research-related data.

Definition:

"A method of data collection in which one person (interviewer) asks the questions from another person (respondent) conducted either face-to-face or telephonically."

Characteristics of interview:

-Characteristics of Interview

-The participants, the interviewer, and the respondent are strangers.

-The relationship between the participants is a transitory one.
-Interview is a mode of obtaining verbal answers to questions put verbally.

- The interaction between the interviewer and the respondent need not necessarily be face to-face because interviews can be conducted over telephone also.

Benefits of interview:

1. provide in depth and detailed information.

2. permits greater depth of response.

3. Data from illiterate subject.

4. higher response.

5. help to gather other supplementary information.

Types of Interview:

1. Structured Interview:

Structured interview is a means of data collection in which the interviewer has an interview schedule in which the questions are listed in the order in which they are to be answered.

2. Unstructured Interview:

These interviews are also known as nonstandardized interviews. Unstructured interview is method wherein the questions can be changed to meet the respondent's intelligence, under standing, and beliefs.

3. semistructured Interview:

Semistructured interview is a flexible method that allows new questions to be brought up during the interview, depending upon the situation during the interview.

4. In-depth Interview:

This is an intensive and investigative interview conducted and aimed at studying the respon dent's opinion and emotions on the basis of interview guide.

5. Focused group Interview:

group Focused interview is an unstructured group interview technique where 8-12 members are brought together under the guidance of a trained interviewer to focus on a specific phenomenon.

6. Telephone Interview:

Telephone interviewing is a nonpersonal method of data collection. This method of collecting information consists of contacting respondents on telephone itself. It is used widely in indus trial surveys, particularly in developed regions.

The Interviewing process are as following:

-Preparation for interview

-Pre-interview introduction.

-Developing rapport

-Carrying the interview forward.

-Recording the interview

- Closing the interview.

The data collection, sources of data collection and methods of data collection are given above.

Q 1. Enumerate the sources of data .

= Data means information that is systematically collected in the courses of study .

DATA SOURCES

Information collected from different research studies generally depends on various sources. However, a quality research study requires that highly reliable and valid data are collected; therefore diligence and application of the researcher can be of high importance. Sources of data collection in different research studies largely depend on several factors such as type of research study, phenomenon under study, purpose of the study, etc. However, basically sources of data are generally categorized in two broad categories, namely primary and secondary sources as discussed below:

Primary sources: Primary data are directly collected from the research units, which may be individuals, objects, programmes, or institutions. Primary sources provide the first-hand information that is collected by the researcher directly from the respondents or the situations, which may be collected through interviews, questioning, observation, biochemical measurements, and psychosocial measurement scales.

Primary sources	Secondary sources		
	Internal sources (Private documents)	External sources (Public documents)	
		Published records	Unpublished records
-People, objects, programmes, institutions, etc. (Primary data are collected through interviews, questioning, observation, biochemical measurements, and psychosocial measurement scales)	-Biographies -Diaries -Letters -Memoires	-Journals & magazines -Newspapers -Government reports -Statistical abstracts -Census reports -Mass communication -Commission reports	-Unpublished thesis -Unpublished dissertations and reports -Official or patient records

sources of data

Secondary sources: Secondary data are collected from either internal or external secondary sources. External sources involve existing material such as published or unpublished records. Published records may include the journals, magazines, newspapers, government reports, statistical abstracts, census reports, constituents of mass communication, and commission reports. Unpublished records may include official records, patient records, thesis, dissertations, and reports. In addition, internal secondary sources also known as private documents may include the biographies, personal diaries, letters, memoires, etc.

Q 2. Methods of Data collections .

= Data means information that is systematically collected in the courses of study .

METHODS OF COLLECTING PRIMARY DATA

Primary data are directly collected by the researcher from their original sources. In this case, the researcher can collect the required data precisely according to his research needs, he can collect them when he wants them and in the form he needs them. But the collection of primary data is costly and time consuming. Yet, for several types of social science research required data are not available form secondary sources and they have to be directly gathered form the primary sources.

In such cases where the available data are inappropriate, inadequate or obsolete, primary data have to be gathered. They include: socio-economic surveys, social anthropological studies of rural communities and tribal communities, sociological studies of social problems and social institutions, nursing research, leadership studies, opinion polls, attitudinal surveys, readership, radio listening and T.V. viewing surveys, knowledge-awareness practice (KAP) studies, nursing management studies, hospital management studies, etc.

There are various methods of data collection. A 'Method' is different from a 'Tool.' While a method refers to the way or mode of gathering data, a tool is an instrument used for the method.

For example, a schedule is used for interviewing. The important methods are **(a) observation, (b) interviewing, (c) mail survey, (d) experimentation, (e) simulation, and (f) projective technique.**

To collect primary data during the course of doing experiments in an experimental research but in case we do research of the descriptive type and perform surveys, whether sample surveys or census surveys, then we can obtain primary data either through observation or through direct communication with respondents in one form or another or through personal interviews.

This, in other words, means that there are several methods of collecting primary data, particularly in surveys and descriptive researches.

Important ones are:

(i) observation method,

(ii) interview method,

(iii) through questionnaires,

(iv) through schedules and

(v) other methods which include

(a) warranty cards;

(b) distributor audits;

(c) pantry audits;

(d) consumer panels;

(e) using mechanical devices;

(f) through projective techniques;

(g) depth interviews, and

(h) content analysis.

Observations involves gathering of data relating to the selected research by viewing and or listening.

Interviewing involves face-to-face conversation between the investigator and the respondent.

Mailing is used for collecting data by getting questionnaires completed respondents.

Experimentation involves a study of independent variables under controlled conditions.

Experiments may be conducted in a laboratory or in field in a natural setting. Simulation involves creation of an artificial situation similar to the actual life situation.

Projective methods aim at drawing inferences on the characteristics of respondents by presenting to them stimuli.

Even method has its advantages and disadvantages.

Q 3 . Discuss on advantages and disadvantages of observation as method of data collection.

= OBSERVATIONS

Observation is a way of gathering data by watching behaviour, events, or noting physical characteristics in their natural setting. Observation is a method of data collection that can be used to gather such information as characteristics and conditions of individual, verbal and nonverbal communication, etc. Observation method of data collection is particularly well suited to nursing research.

There are several situations that require nurses to use the observation method for data collection such as behaviour and attributes of the patients, their families, and hospital staff, and so on.

Observations can be overt (everyone knows they are being observed) or covert (they do not know that they are being observed and the observer is concealed). The benefit of covert observation is that people are more likely to behave naturally if they do not know that they are being observed.

Definitions

Observation is a technique for collecting all the data or acquiring information through occurrences that can be observed through senses with or without mechanical devices.

It is a two part process to collect data for study that includes an observer (someone who is observing) and the observed (there is something to observe).

Advantages of Observation

- Collect data where and when an event or activity is occurring.
- Does not rely on people's willingness or ability to provide information.
- Allows you to directly see what people do rather than relying on what people say they did.

Disadvantages of Observation

- Susceptible to observer bias.
- Susceptible to the 'Hawthorne effect', that is, people usually perform better when they know they are being observed, although indirect observation may decrease this problem.
- Can be expensive and time-consuming compared to other data collection
- Does not increase understanding of why people behave as they do.

Q 3. LIKERT SCALE

= Likert scale was named after a psychologist Rensis Likert, who developed it in 1932 as a psychological concept measurement scale. Likert scale is one of the most commonly used scaling techniques.

It was developed to measure the attitudes, values, and feelings of people. Primarily original version of this scale was developed with five-point scale (strongly agree, agree, uncertain, disagree, and strongly disagree) containing the mixture of positive and negative declarative statements regarding measuring variables.

An example of 5 points likert's scale may be perused from Table

Table 9.3 Example of five-point Likert scale to assess the attitude with HIV/AIDS
Note. Please tick (✓) in appropriate column for each statement

Statement	Strongly agree	Agree	Uncertain	Disagree	Strongly disagree
1. Person with multiple sex partners is at high risk of AIDS					
2. You can get AIDS by sharing utensils					
3. You may get HIV by sharing needles with others					
4. Only gay men can get AIDS					
5. One way of the getting AIDS is infected blood transfusion					
6. AIDS is a curable disease					

LIKERT SCALE

Definition:

Likert scale is a composite measurement scale use to measure attitude, value, and, feeling of the people that

involve summation of sources on the set of positive and negative declarative statements regarding measuring

variables to which respondents are ask to indicate their degree of agreement or disagreement

Use Of Likert Scale:

1) Use to measure the attitudes, values, feelings of the peoples specific concepts, such as situations, people,

places,objects

2) Use to assess the opinions of respondent about particular concept.

3) it collects the opinion of people with various attitude, emotion and feelings toward a particular concept.

Characteristics Of Likert Scale

1. Psychologic measurement tool: une as psychologic measurement tool to assess the attitudes, and feeling of
people about a specific concept.

2. Neutral statements: This must contain neutral statements.

3. Bipolar scaling method: This composed of alternative positive and negative declarative statement so that
respondent's respond, bias can be eliminated. Here positive statement gets high score with agreement and negative
score gets high score with statement.

4. Measurement of specific number of scaling categories: This scale was originally developed with five scaling
categories; but later scale even developed with four, six and seven scaling categories.

SCORING OF THE LIKERT SCALE

Scoring of the likert scale is done on the bias of type of statement and level of respondents agreement with
statement. For positive statement respondent get higher score if there is agreement with statement. However in
case of negative statement respondent gets higher score if there is a disagreement with statement.

Advantages Of Likert Scale

1. Its relatively easy to construct this scale.

2. It considered as more reliable and valid tool to measure the psychosocial variables.

3. It is easy to administer, since respondent only have to tick in space provided against of each statement

4. It is less time-consuming during construction and administration.

Disadvantages Of Likert Scale

1. In this scale respondent may feel forced to answer the question.against all preplanned items and their categories.

2. Feelings of the respondent not fully assessed.

3. Difficulty in justifying the selection of the number of categories.

4. Difficult to treat neutral opinions as neither agree or disagree.

Q 4. RATING SCALE

= Rating is the term used to express the opinion or judgement regarding some performance of a person, object, situation, or character. The rating scale involves qualitative description of a limited number of aspects of a thing or traits of a person.

When we use rating scales we judge an object in absolute terms against some specified criteria, i.e. we judge properties of objects without reference to other similar objects.

Definitions

Nursing Research and Statistics Rating scale refers to a scale with a set ofopinion, which describes varying degree of the dimensions of an attitude being observed. Rating scale is devices by which judgements may be qualified or an opinion concerning a trait can be systematized.

Rating scale is a tool in which the one person simply checks off another person's level of performance.

Rating scale could be 3-point, 5-point, or 7-point rating scale. As presented in Figure 9.4 and Figure 9.5..

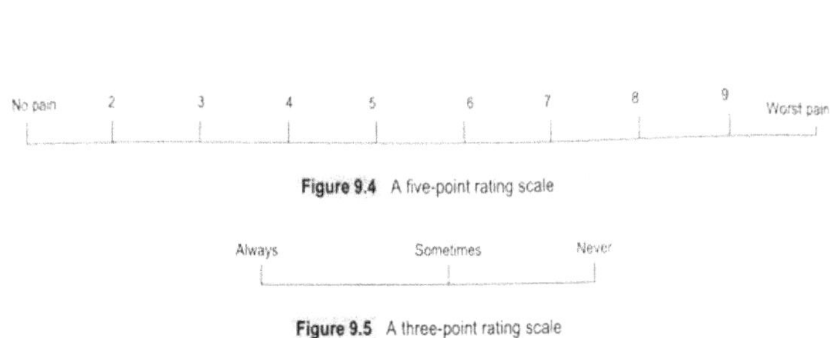

Figure 9.4 A five-point rating scale

Figure 9.5 A three-point rating scale

RATING SCALE

Types of the Rating Scales

1. Graphic rating scale: In this scale the performance is printed horizontally at various points from lowest to highest. It includes the numerical points on the scale.

It is anchored by two extremes presented to respondents for evaluation of a concept or object.

Graphic rating scale

For example: How much are you satisfied with noise control in your ward?

2. Descriptive rating scales: This type of rating scales do not use number, but divide the assessment into series of verbal phrases to indicate the level of performance.

For example: Q. Judge the level ofperformance of nursing personnel in Medical ICU

Nursing personnel in a ward	Level of clinical performance			
	Very active	Active	Moderately active	Passive
1. Amandeep				
2. Jasveen				
3. Tanu				
4. Kirandeep				

Descriptive rating scales

3. Numerical rating scale: It divides the evaluation criteria into a fixed number of points, but defines only numbers at the extremes. In these scales, each statement is generally assigned a numerical score ranging from 1 to 10 or even more.

For example: Pain assessment numerical scale.

Numerical rating scale

4. Comparative rating scale: In this type of rating scale, the researcher makes a judgement about an attribute of a person by comparing it with that of a similar another person(s).

For example, Mr. Ram's decision-making abilities closely resemble those of Mr. Shyam and Mr. Gopal. In this type of rating scale, researcher must have prehand knowledge about the selected attributes of the people with whom the subjects are suppose to be compared.

RATING SCALE

Definitions

1) Rating scale refers to a scale with a set of opinion, which describes varying degree of the dimensions of an attitude
being observed.

2) Rating scale is a device by which judgements may be qualified or an opinion concerning a trait can be
systematized.

Types of the Rating Scale

1. Graphic rating scale.

In this scale, the performance is printed horizontally at various points from lowest to highest. It includes the numerical points on the scale. It is anchored by two extremes presented to respondents for evaluation of a concept or object.

2. Descriptive rating scales:

This type of rating scales do not use number, but divide the assessment into series of verbal phrases to indicate the level of performance.

3. Numerical rating scale:

It divides the evaluation criteria into a fixed number of points, but defines only numbers at the extremes. In these scales, each statement is generally assigned a numerical score ranging from 1 to 10, or even more.

4. Comparative rating scale.

In this type of rating scale, the researcher makes a judgement about an attribute of a person by comparing it with that of a similar another person(s) For example, Mr. Ram's decision-making abilities closely resemble those of Mr. Shyam and Mr. Gopal. In this type of rating scale, researcher must have prehand knowledge about the selected attributes of the people with whom the subjects are supposed to be compared

Characteristics of Rating Scale

1) Rating scale is the judgement of one person by another

2) It is a directed observation

3) It is opinion of some object, situation or character

4)it systemizes the expression of opinion concerning a trait.

5) a systematic procedure for obtaining, recording and reporting observer's judgements.

6) it is a subjective method through which we can find out opinions about a particular person.

7) similar to a check list but with finer discriminations.

8) it may be filled during or immediately after or much later after the observation is made.

9) ratings are done by parents, guardians, teachers, students themselves, friends, a board of interviewers, judges, and by the self as well.

10) each statement constructed in rating scale must be unique in itself so that attributes can be judged appropriately.

Advantages Of Rating Scale

1) easy to administer and score the measured attributes.

2) rating scales have a wide range of application in nursing research

3) graphic rating scale is easier to make and requires less time.

4) rating scales can be easily used for a large group.

5) it is also used for quantitative methods.

6) it may also be used for the assessment of interests, attitudes, and personnel characteristics.

7) used to evaluate performance, skills, and product outcomes.

8) rating scales are adaptable and flexible research instruments.

Disadvantages Of Rating Scale

1) it is difficult or dangerous to fix up rating about many aspects of an individual.

2) misuse can result in decrease in objectivity.

3) there are chances of subjective evaluation, thus the scales may become unscientific and unreliable.

4) limited reliability

5) may be substantial variations among informants

6) do not assess sources of behavior problems

7) ease of use - unqualified users may use and interpret these scales.

8) not suitable for sophisticated treatment planning

CHAPTER THIRTEEN

Analysis of Data

Q 1. Data presentation and Interpretation.

= Data presentation and analysis plays an essential role in every field. An excellent presentation can be a deal maker or deal breaker. Some people make an increasable useful presentation with the same set of facts and figures which are available with others.

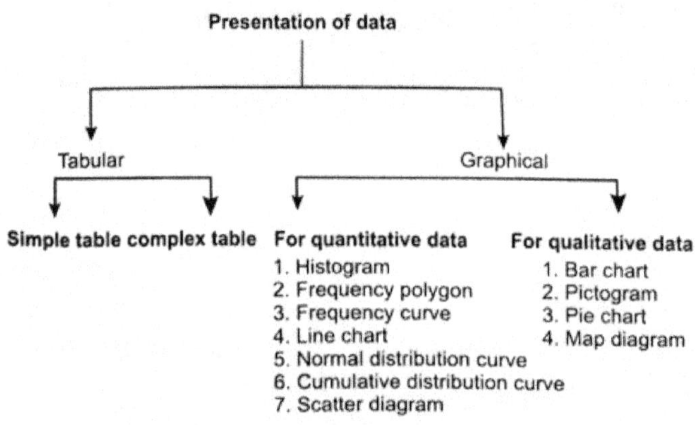

Presentation of data

1. Presentation of data is generally done by these two methods:

a. Tabular presentation,

b. presentation

2. Tabulated data will give some information and also allow for further analysis.

3. The columns and rows in a table make eye strain and there are chances of poor visual impression of data presented in a tabular form.

4. In such circumstances data can be presented in the form of picture, diagram or figure which will help in good comparison through good visual impression.

5. The graphs and diagrams are of utmost importance in creating interest from the observational data.

6. One should take care to select major data presentable in graph or diagram.

7. The presentation of data by diagram proves a very considerable aid and has much to commend it, if certain basic principles are not forgotten.

8. Main objective of diagram is to help the eye to grasp series of numbers and to grasp the meaning of series of data and also to assist the intelligence.

STATISTICS

STATISTICS

Q 1. Explain the uses and application of statistics in nursing.

= DEFINITION

1. Statistics can be defined as the collection presentation and interpretation of numerical data.- **Croxton and Crowed.**

2. Statistics are numerical statement of facts in any department of enquiry placed interrelation to each other.- **Bouly**

Application of statistics in nursing..

1. To find out the growth rate, the fertility status and the population size of the country.

2. It facilitates to know about health status of the community.

3. To assess the adequacy of the medical and paramedical manpower and of the health institutions in the country

4.To look for the differences in the magnitude of disease by person, place and time. .

5. Statistics helps in providing a better understanding and exact description of a phenomenon of nature.

6. Statistical helps in proper and efficient planning of a statistical inquiry in any field of study.

7. Statistical helps in collecting an appropriate quantitative data.

8. Statistics helps in presenting complex data in a suitable tabular, diagrammatic and graphic form for an easy and clear comprehension of the data.

9. Statistics helps in understanding the nature and pattern of variability of a phenomenon through quantitative observations.

10. Statistics helps in drawing valid inference, along with a measure of their reliability about the population parameters from the sample data.

Q 2. Functions of statistics

= 1. Expression of facts in numbers - One of the main function of Statistics is to express numbers in easily understandable language and interpret the results with certainty.

2. Simple presentation - Statistics enables presentation of complex data in a simple format in terms of aggregate, average, percentage, graphs, diagrams etc.

3. Enlarges individual knowledge and experience - Statistics expands the horizons of individual knowledge and understanding.

4. It compares facts - It facilitates the comparison of data and identifying the interrelations between large sets of data for drawing suitable inferences.

5. Facilitates policy formulation - By doing analysis and interpretation fo data, precise nature of problem can be ascertained thus assisting policy formulation.

6. It helps other science in testing their laws - Statistics helps other laws for establishing their assumptions. E.g., many laws of economics namely law of demand, law of supply, Keynes theory of employment can be verified by Statistics.

7. It helps in forecasting - Extrapolating present data aids in forecasting likely changes that can be expected in future.

Q 3. Explain the most commonly used measures of dispersion.

= METHODS OF DISPERSION

Methods of studying dispersion are divided into two types :

i. Mathematical Methods: We can study the 'degree' and 'extent' of variation by these methods. In this category, commonly used measures of dispersion are: a. Range

b. Quartile Deviation

c. Average Deviation

d. Standard deviation and coefficient of variation.

=

Dispersion is another analytical method to study data.

A main use of dispersion is to compare the amounts of spread in two (or more) data sets.

A common technique in inferential statistics is to draw comparisons between populations by analyzing samples that come from those populations.

Two of the most common measures of dispersion are the *range* and the *standard deviation*.

Range

For any set of data, the **range** of the set is given by the following formula:

Range = (greatest value in set) – (least value in set).

=

Range

Example:

The two sets below have the same mean and median (7). Find the range of each set.

Set A	1	2	7	12	13
Set B	5	6	7	8	9

Range of Set A: 13 – 1 = 12

Range of Set A: 9 – 5 = 4

One of the most useful measures of dispersion is the ***standard deviation.***

It is based on ***deviations from the mean*** of the data.

Find the deviations from the mean for all data values of the sample 1, 2, 8, 11, 13.

The mean is 7.

To find each deviation, subtract the mean **from** each data value.

Data Value	1	2	8	11	13
Deviation	-6	-5	1	4	6

The sum of the deviations is always equal to zero.

Calculating the Sample Standard Deviation

$$s = \sqrt{\frac{\sum (x - \bar{x})^2}{n-1}}.$$

The **sample standard deviation** is found by calculating the square root of the **variance**.

The **variance** is found by summing the squares of the deviations and dividing that sum by $n - 1$ (since it is a sample instead of a population).

The sample standard deviation is denoted by the letter s.

The standard deviation of a population is denoted by σ.

1. Calculate the mean of the numbers.

2. Find the deviations from the mean.

3. Square each deviation.

4. Sum the squared deviations.

5. Divide the sum in Step 4 by $n - 1$.

6. Take the square root of the quotient in Step 5.

Standard Deviation

Calculating the Sample Standard Deviation

Example:

Find the standard deviation of the sample set $\{1, 2, 8, 11, 13\}$.

$\bar{x} = (1+2+8+11+13)/5 = 7$

Data Value	1	2	8	11	13
Deviation	-6	-5	1	4	6
$(\text{Deviation})^2$	36	25	1	16	36

Sum of the $(\text{Deviations})^2 = 36 + 25 + 1 + 16 + 36 = 114$

Sum of the (Deviations)^2 = $36 + 25 + 1 + 16 + 36 =$ 114

Divide 114 by $n - 1$ with $n = 5$:

$$\frac{114}{5 - 1} = 28.5$$

Take the square root of 28.5:

$$\sqrt{28.5} = 5.34$$

The sample standard deviation of the data is 5.34.

Q4. Explain the uses and sources of the vital statistics.

= Vital statistics are statistics on live births, deaths, fetal deaths, marriages and divorces. The most common way of collecting information on these events is through civil registration an administrative system used by governments to record vital events which occur in their populations.

Efforts to improve the quality of vital statistics will therefore be closely related to the development of civil registration systems in countries.

Defination

Vital statistics are conventionally numerical records of marriage, births, sickness and deaths by which the health and growth of community may be studied.

Vital statistics is a part of demography and collective study of mankind. It deals with the data's related to vital events.

Uses of vital statistics

1. Vital statistics shows changing pattern of the population of a country. (medical / facilities, standard of living, etc)

2. Manufacturers plan their production by using vital statistics. (food, clothing etc.)

3. Birth and death certificates are needed in many circumstances.

4. Accurately registered and systematically collected vital statistics can be used to check up the accuracy of data provided by the census.

5. The vital statistics are the administrative ad research needs of public health agencies.

For the Individual

1. Vital statistics are of much use for an individual.

2. A birth certificate issued by the registering authority is an important document which records the date, time, place and parentage of the person.

3. It establishes his identity as the citizen of the country.

4. It is a legal document which is used for admission to a school, for getting a passport to travel abroad and even to migrate to another country, etc.

5. Similarly, a marriage certificate records the marital status of a couple and legalises the birth of children from that marriage.

Legal Use

1. Vital statistics are legally very useful.

2. Certificates relating to birth, death, marriage, divorce, etc. have legal importance.

3. For instance, a death certificate is an important legal document for the settlement of property of the deceased person, the claim of his/her insurance policy, etc.

Health and Family Planning Programmes

1. Vital statistics relating to births and deaths can be used in health and family planning programmes of the government.

2. The causes of deaths, and the mortality rates of different categories help in assessing the health condition of the people.

3. Accordingly, the state can formulate such health programmes as malaria eradication, polio and small pox immunisation, tuberculosis, etc.

4. In keeping with the requirements of the population, the government can open hospitals, maternity and child welfare centres, etc.

Study of Social Conditions

Vital statistics like birth and death rates, divorce rate, widow remarriage, widowhood, etc. throw light on the social conditions of a society, as also its customs and traditions.

For Administrators and Planners

Data provided by vital statistics relating to trend and growth of population in the various age groups and on the whole, help planners and administrators to plan and formulate policies for public health, education, housing, transport and communications, food supplies, etc.

For the Nation

1. Vital statistics are of much importance for the nation.

2. They help in analyzing the population trends at any given point of time.

3. They try to fill the gap between two censuses.

4. They relate to the composition, size, distribution and growth of populatio

5. It is on their basis that population projections can be made.

6. Vital statistics help in formulating policies for providing social security to the people.

7. Even the rules for immigration and emigration can be framed on the basis of population growth data.

8. Vital statistics are also used for updating electoral rolls and demarcation of constituencies.

SOURCES OF VITAL STATISTICS

There are four major sources of vital statistics namely;

a. The Sample Registration System (,SRS)

b. The Civil Registration System (CRS),

c. Indirect estimates from the decennial census and

d. Indirect estimates from the National Family Health Surveys (NFHS).

The SRS is the most regular source of demographic statistics in India. It is based on a system of dual recording of births and deaths in fairly representative sample units spread all over the country.

The SRS provides annual estimates of

a. Population composition,

b. Fertility,

c. Mortality, and

d. Medical attention at the time of birth or death which give some idea about access to medical care.

Q 5. Scales of Measurements .

= In statistics and quantitative research methodology, various attempts have been made to classify variables (or types of data) and thereby develop taxonomy of levels of measurement or scales of measure.

Perhaps the best known are those developed by the psychologist Stanley Smith Stevens.

He proposed four types: **nominal, ordinal, interval, and ratio.**

DEFINITION

Measurements are the process of assigning numbers to variables. Measurements, as used in research, imply the qualification of information that is the assigning of some types of numbers to data.

LEVELS OF MEASUREMENT

The level of measurement describes the relationship among these three values.

1. **Ordinal measurements:-** it involves the sorting of objects on the basis of their relative standing to each other on a specified attribute.

2. **Interval measurement:** it indicates not only rank ordering of objects on an attribute but also the amount of distance between each object. Distance between numberic values on the interval scale represents equivalent distance in the attribute being measured.

3. **Nominal measurement:** are distinguished interval measurement by virtue of having a rational zero point. Most sophisticated statistical procedures require measures on the interval or ratio scales.

Distance, age, time, weight, strength, blood pressure	Numbers represent units with equal intervals, measured from true zero	
Calendar years, IQ, degrees centigrade or Fahrenheit	Equal intervals between numbers, but not related to true zero; therefore, not representing absolute quantity	Int
Manual muscle test, functional status, pain	Numbers indicate rank order of observations	Ordinal
Sex, nationality, blood type, clinical diagnosis	Numerals represent category lables only, classification	Nominal

4. Ratio measurement there is always an absolute zero that is meaningful. This means that you can construct a meaningful fraction (or ratio) with a ratio variable. Weight is a ratio variable.

Stevens (1946) classified variables into four levels. These are referred to as level of measurement or levels of data.

1. Nominal
2. Ordinal
3. Interval Scale
4. Ratio Scale

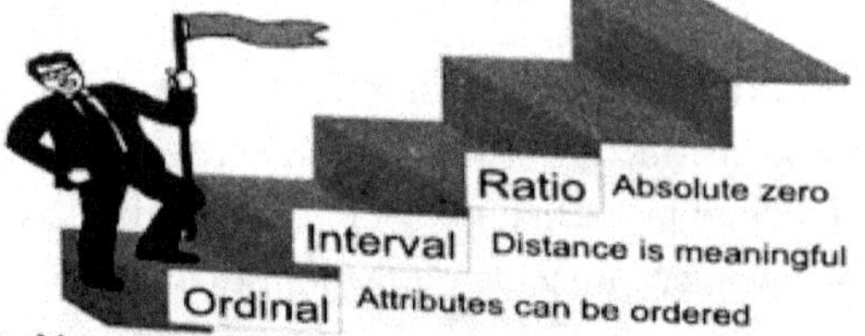

Fig. 27.3 : Four leivels of measurement

Table · 27.1 : Levels of Measurement

Incremental Progress	Measure property	Mathematical Operators	Advanced Operations	Central Tendency
Nominal	Classification, membership	=, !=	Grouping	mode
Ordinal	Comparison, Level	>, <	Sorting	Median
Interval	Difference, Affinity	+, -	Yardstick	Mean, Deviation
Ratio	Magnitude, Amount	+, /	Ratio	Geometric Mean, Coeff. of Variation

Levels of Measurements.

FUNCTIONS OF MEASUREMENT

Measurements is widely used for

1. Selection of personnel in industry / institution.

2. Various types of classification effectively.

3. In order to compare two individuals.

4. In research, it is basic part of research.

5. Improving classroom instruction.

Q 6. Measurement of central tendancy.

= Measures of central tendency are used to describe what is normal for a set of data. Mean, median, and mode are the three measures of central tendency. The mode can be used with both numerical and nominal data The term central tendency refers to the "middle" value or perhaps a typical value of the data, and is measured using the mean, median, or mode. Each of these measures is calculated differently, and the one that is best to use depends upon the situation. The central tendency otherwise called statistical averages. The word "average" implies a value in the distribution, around which the other values are distributed.

Mean

The average value

How to find the mean:

1. Add up all the numbers.
2. Divide the sum by the number of values.

E.g. The mean of 3,2,10,5 is

$$\frac{3+2+10+5}{4} = \frac{20}{4} = 5$$

Median

The middle number

How to find the Median:

1. Put the numbers from smallest to largest.
2. The number in the middle is the median. If there are two middle numbers, add them and divide by two.

Mode

The most frequent number

Special Cases:

- **No mode** if all the numbers occur the same amount of times.
- **More than one mode** if more than one number is the most frequent.

Range

Difference between highest and lowest numbers

How to find the Range:

1. Put the numbers from Smallest to largest.
2. Subtract the lowest value from the largest.

Measurement of central tendancy.

DEFINITION

1. Central tendency isdefined as "the statistical measure that identifies a single value as representative of an entire distribution."

2. Central tendency aims to provide an accurate description of the entire data. It is the single value that is most typical/representative of the collected data

MEANING OF CENTRAL TENDENCY

1. A measure of central tendency is a single value that attempts to describe a set of data by identifying the central position within that set of data.

2. Measures of central tendency are sometimes called measures of central location.

3. They are also classed as summary statistics.

4. The mean (often called the average) is most likely the measure of central tendency that you are most familiar with, but there are others, such as the median and the mode.

5. The mean, median and mode are all valid measures of central tendency, but under different conditions, some measures of central tendency become more appropriate to use than others.

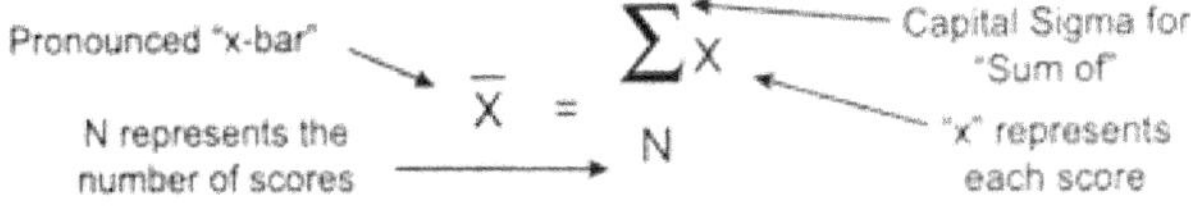

Characteristics

The important characteristics for an ideal measure of central tendency are

I . It should be based on all the observations of the series.

ii. It should be easy to calculate and simple to understand.

iii. It should not be affected by extreme values.

iv. It should be rigidly defined..

V. It should be capable of further mathematical treatment

vi. It should be least affected by the fluctuations of sampling.

Q 7. Advantages and disadvantages of Mean , Medium.

=

: Merits and demerits of means median	
Mean	**Median**
Use the mean to describe the middle of a set of data that does not have an outlier.	Use the median to describe the middle of a set of data that does have an outlier.
Advantages	**Advantages**
• Most popular measure in fields such as business, engineering and computer science.	• Extreme values (outliers) do not affect the median as strongly as they do the mean.
• It is unique - there is only one answer.	• Useful when comparing sets of data.
• Useful when comparing sets of data.	• It is unique - there is only one answer.
Disadvantages	**Disadvantages**
• Affected by extreme values (outliers)	• Not as popular as mean.

Advantages and disadvantages of Mean , Medium.

Q 8. Normal probability curve.

= In probability theory, the normal (or Gaussian) distribution is a very commonly occurring continuous probability distribution-a function that tells the probability that any real observation will fall between any two real limits or real numbers, as the curve approaches zero on either side.

CONCEPTS OF NORMAL DISTRIBUTION

1. The curve is a symmetrical, bell-shaped curve with the highest frequency occurring in the middle and gradually tapering toward the extremes.

2. In a normal distribution, 68.2% of all scores cluster around the mean within approximately 1 standard deviation, 95.4% within approximately 2 standard deviations, and 99.7% within approximately 3 standard deviations.

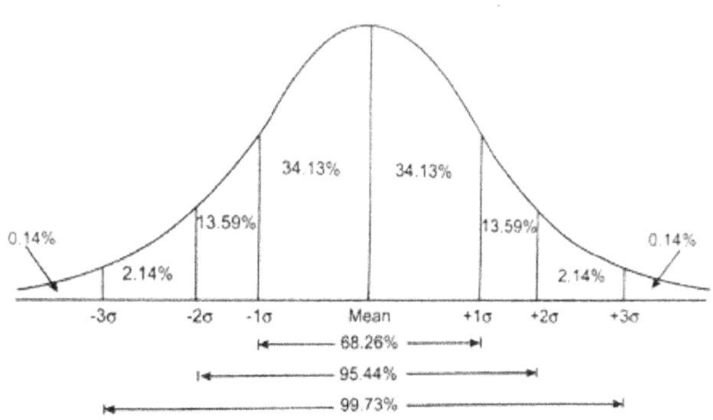

Fig. 29.6 : The percentage of the cases falling between successive Standard deviations in normal distribution

3. It also called normal curve, Gauss' curve.

4. The normal distribution (often referred to as the "bell curve" is at the core of most of inferential statistics.

5. By assuming that most complex processes result in a normal distribution (we'll see why this is reasonable), we can gauge the probability of it happening by chance.

6. To best enjoy this tutorial, it is good to come to it understanding what probability distributions and random variables are.

Characteristics of normal curve.

1.It will be bell shaped.

2. It is symmetrical in distribution on either side of mean are equal in number.

3.It has maximum height is at the mean.

4. Mean, median and mode are coinciding.

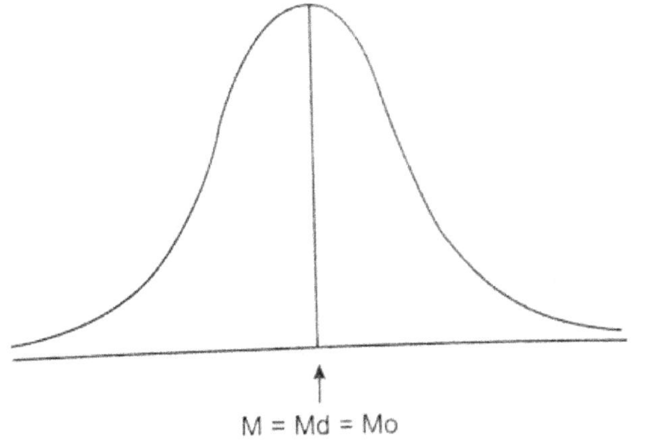

5. It is asymptomatic (the tails never touch the base line theoretically)

6. It has two curves - central part convex - when come down, it becomes concave on both sides.

7. The normal probability curve is continuous type probability curve.

8. All the measures of central tendency are equal meland suitable on the highest peak axis (i.e., mean = median = mode) -

9. The total area under the curve is equal to unity.

10. The normal curve has two parameter i.e., mean and standard deviation.

IMPORTANCE OF NORMAL PROBABILTY CURVE

1. The normal distribution is important is that many psychological and educational variables are distributed approximately normally.

2. Measures of reading ability, introversion, job satisfaction, and memory are among the many psychological variables approximately normally distributed. although the distributions are only approximately normal, they are usually quite close.

3. It is very helpful in forecasting .We can calculate the estimated length of the bones of animals and woods and leaves. Because if animals are one type their numbering is normally distributed.

4. The normal distribution is so important is that it is easy for mathematical statisticians to work with.

5. Normal distribution is very useful for controlling the quality in business. With this we can fix the limit of quality. that will helpful for controlling the quality.

6. If we take one sample out of the universe and calculate the mean size of growing then it will normal distribution

7. This means that many kinds of statistical tests can be derived for normal distributions.

8. Almost all statistical tests discussed in this text assume normal distributions.

9. These tests work very well even if the distribution is only approximately normally distributed. Some tests work well even with very wide deviations from normality.

10. If the mean and standard deviation of a normal distribution are known, it is easy to convert back and forth from raw scores to percentiles.

Q 9. Type-1 and -II Errors

= Type-1 and -II Errors

Type-I error occurs when null hypothesis is rejected, when it should have been accepted; also called alpha error. Type-II error occurs where null hypothesis is accepted, when it should actually have been rejected. It is also known as beta error. These errors generally occur due to unrepresentative sample drawn from the population .

Q 10.Level of Significance

= Probability of making type-I error is called as level of significance. It is represented by a or the p. In other words, level of significance is probability of rejecting the null hypothesis when it is true. In health sciences, we generally consider the level of significance either 1% (.01) or the 5% (.05).

A significance of .05 means that the researcher is willing to take risk being wrong 5% of the times, 5 times out 100, when rejecting the null hypothesis.

If the decision needs to be much more accurate, such as deciding if a nursing intervention is effective or not, the level of significance might be set at .01 or even at .001. With a .01 level of significance, the researcher stands the risk of being wrong 1 time out of 100 when rejecting the null hypothesis.

At the .001 level of significance, the risk is 1 time out of 1,000. However, most of the nursing studies consider .05 level of significance to take a decision regarding whether to accept or reject the null hypotheses.

Q 11. DESCRIPTIVE AND INFERENTIAL STATISTICS

= statistics is broadly classified in two categories, i.e. descriptive and inferential. Descriptive statistics deal with the enumeration, organization, and graphical representation of data. An example of descriptive statistics is the decennial census of India, in which all the residents are requested to provide information such as age, gender, religion, marital status, education, and occupation.

The data obtained in such a census can be compiled and arranged into tables and graphs that describe characteristics of the population at a given time. Inferential statistics provides the procedures draw an inference about the conditions that exist in a large set of observations, i.e. an entire population from study of a part of that set (sample).

This branch of statistics is also known as sampling statistics. An example of inferential static is to test the efficacy of a new antihypertensive drug in which the physician will have only a limited number of hypertensive subjects on which efficacy is tested and inferences are drawn.

DESCRIPTIVE STATISTICS :

Descriptive statistics are used to organize and summarize data to draw meaningful interpretations. Descriptive statistics also allow the researcher to interpret the data meaningfully, so that research questions can be answered completely and appropriately. Descriptive statistics may be categorized in several ways; however, this chapter presents the most simplified classification of the descriptive statistics that includes:

Frequency distribution and graphical presentation (measures of condensation)

Measures of central tendency

Measures of dispersion

Measures of relationship (correlation coefficient)

Q 12.Frequency Distribution

= An appropriate presentation of data involves organization of data in such a manner that meaningful conclusions and inferences can drawn to answer the research question. Unsorted and ungrouped records do not allow us to draw clear conclusion. Quantitative data are generally condensed and frequency distribution is presented through tables, charts, graphs, and diagrams.

Tables: A table presents data in a concise, systematic manner from masses of statistical data. Tabulation is the first step before data is used for further statistical analysis and interpretation. Tabulation means a systematic presentation of information contained in the data in rows and columns in accordance with some features and characteristics. Rows are horizontal and columns are vertical arrangements.

Q 12. Types and graph in data presentation

= Graphical presentation of data:

The main reasons for using the diagrammatic and graphic representation of data are as follows:

- They are the most convenient and appealing ways in which statistical results may be presented.
- They give an overall view of entire data. They are visually more attractive than other ways of representing data.
- It is easier to understand and memorize data through graphical representation.

- They facilitate comparison of data relating to different periods of time of different origins.

Types of diagram and graphs: The commonly used diagrams and graphs in the presentation of data of the research studies are bar diagram, pie diagram, histogram, frequency polygon, line graphs, cumulative frequency curve, scattered diagrams, pictograms, and map diagrams.

Bar diagram: It is a convenient, graphical device that is particularly useful for displaying nominal or ordinal data. It is an easy method adopted for visual comparison of the magnitude of different frequencies. Length of the bars drawn vertically or horizontally indicates the frequency of a character. The bar charts are called vertical bar charts (or column charts) if the bars are placed vertically. When the bars are placed horizontally, we get horizontal bar charts. There are three types of bar diagrams:

1. Simple bar diagram
2. Multiple bar diagram
3. Proportion bar diagram .

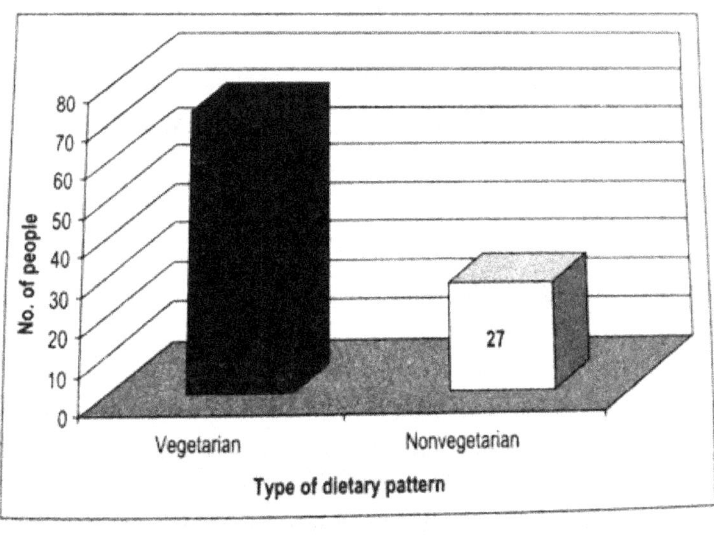

Figure Simple bar diagram showing dietary pattern of people

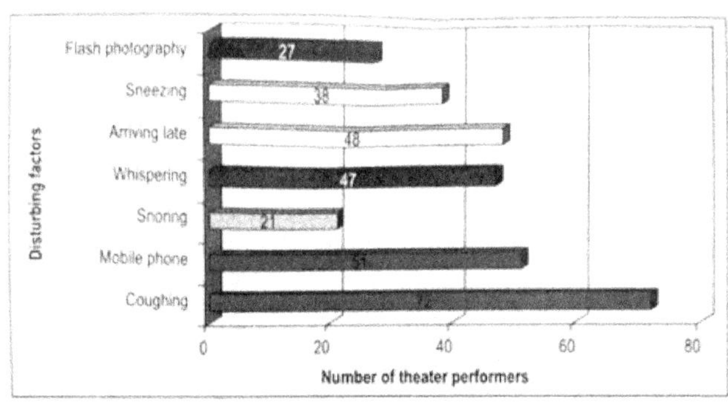

Multiple bar diagram showing disturbing factors experienced by theatre performers during their theatre performance.

Pie diagram/sector diagram: It is another useful pictorial device for presenting discrete data of qualitative characteristics such as age groups, genders, and occupational groups in a population .

The total area of the circle represents the entire data under consideration.

Researcher must remember that only percentage data must be used to prepare pie diagrams. It gives comparative differences at a glance . size of each angle is calculated by multiple class percentages with a 360 or formula may at be a used that .

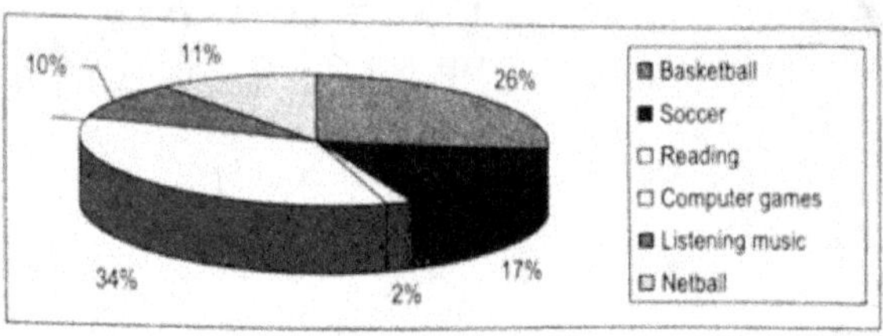

Figure   Pie diagram showing cultural and leisure activities in which urban children participate

Histogram: It is the most commonly used graphical representation of grouped frequency distribution. Variable characters of the different groups are indicated on the horizontal line (x-axis) and frequencies (number of observation) are indicated on the vertical line (y-axis). Frequency of each group forms a column or rectangle. Such diagram is called 'histogram'.

The area of rectangle is proportional to the frequency of the correspondence class interval, and the total area of the histogram being proportional to the total frequency of all the class intervals. A histogram may be drawn by using following steps:

1. Set of vertical bars the areas of which are proportional to frequencies represented.
2. The difference of histogram from bar diagram is that bar diagram is one dimensional and only the length of the bar has its significance while in histograms both length and width matters.
3. When class intervals are equal, frequency is taken on y-axis, the variables on x-axis, and adjacent rectangles are constructed.
4. When the class intervals are unequal, a correction for unequal class intervals must be made.

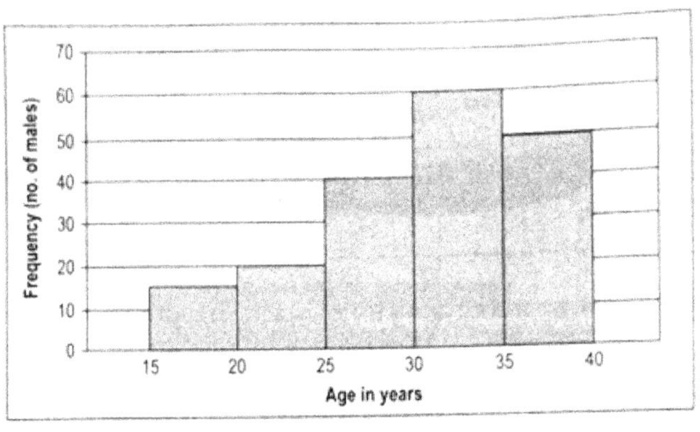

Figure   Histogram depicting number of males in different age groups

Frequency polygon: It is the curve obtained by joining the midpoints of the tops of the rectangles points of the line drawn are joined to the horizontal axis at the midpoint of the empty class-intervals histogram by straight lines. It gives a polygon, i.e. figure with many angles. In this, the two end data pattern more clearly than histograms. On the same axis one can plot frequency polygons of both ends of the frequency distribution. Frequency polygons are simple and sketch an outline of Several distributions, thereby making comparisons possible. A histogram can be drawn by using following stapes :

- Draw the histogram of given data.
- Join the midpoints ofupper horizontal sides of each rectangle with the adjacent one by a straight line.
- Close the polygon at the both ends of distribution by extending them to base line.
- Hypothetical classes at the each end would have to be included at each end with a frequency of zero.

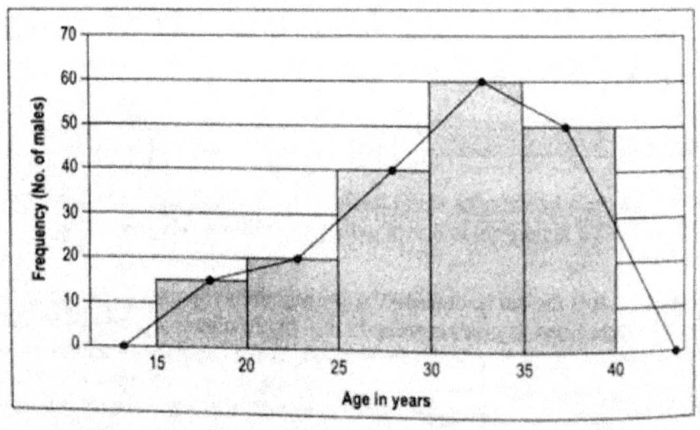

Figure   Frequency polygon depicting number of males in different age groups

Line graphs: In this, variables in the frequency polygon are depicting by line. It is mostly used where data is collected over a long period of time. On x-axis, values of independent variables are taken and values of dependent variables are taken on y-axis.

Vertical axis may not start from zero, but at some point, from where frequency starts. With reference to x- and y-axis, the given data may be plotted and these consecutive points or data are then joined by straight line.

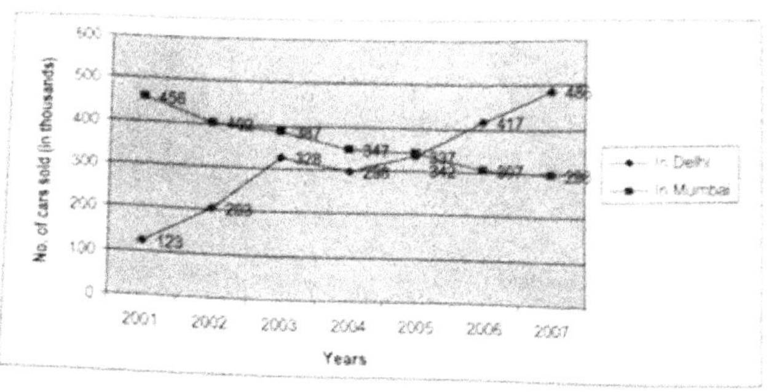

Figure Line graph presenting the number of cars sold in Delhi and Mumbai during 2001–2007

Cumulative frequency curve or ogive: This graph represents the data of a cumulative frequency distribution. For drawing an ogive, an ordinary frequency distribution table is converted into cumulative Frequency table.

The cumulative frequencies are then plotted corresponding to the upper limits of the classes. The points corresponding to cumulative frequency at each upper limit of the classes are joined a free-hand curve. The diagram made is called **ogive**.

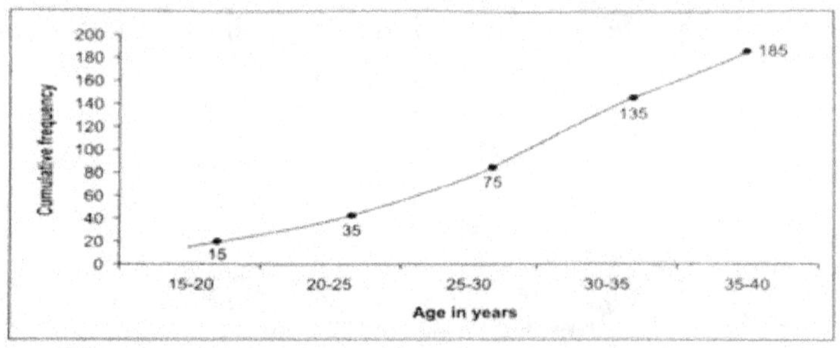

Figure Cumulative frequency curve presenting number of males in different age groups

Scattered or dotted diagrams: It is a graphic presentation that shows the nature of correlation between two variable characters x and y on the similar features or characteristics, e.g. height and weight 20 years old. Therefore, it is also called correlation diagram.

Example of a scattered or doctored grams is presented in Figure

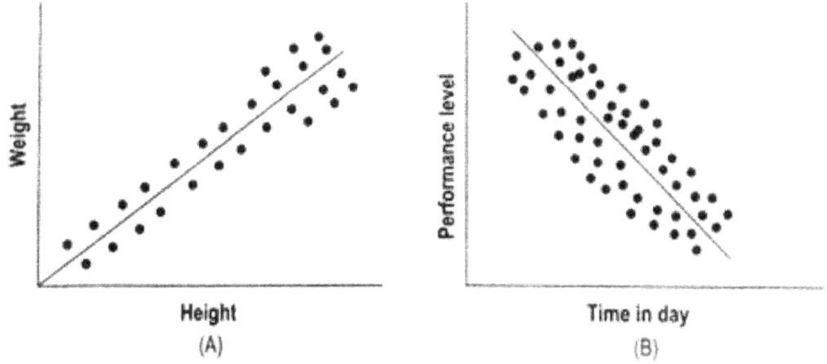

Figure Scattered diagram showing (A) positive correlation and (B) negative correlation

Pictograms or picture diagram: This method is used to impress the frequency of the occurrence of events to common people, such as attacks, deaths, number of operations, admissions, accidents, and discharges in a population.

Map diagram or spot map: These maps are prepared to show geographical distribution of frequencies of characteristics.

Limitations of graphs

- Confusing (may be false or true).
- Present only quantitative aspect.
- Get information only on one aspect or on limited characteristics.
- They can present only approximate values.

Q 13. Degree of Freedom

= The interpretation of a statistical test depends on the degree of freedom. It is denoted by the abbreviation 'df' and a number (e.g. df=3). Degree of freedom indicates the number of values that are free to vary. Although the degree of freedom indicates the number of values that can vary, the concern is really focused on the number of values that are not free to vary. The procedure to calculate the degree of freedom varies from test to test; further details are discussed with individual test of significance, and can be referred from there.

Q 14. Tests of Significance

= There are several parametric (t-test, Z-test, ANOVA) and nonparametric tests (chi-square test, median test, McNemar test, Mann-Whitney Test, Wilcoxon Test, Fisher's exact test) available to establish the statistical significance.

Parametric tests: These tests are also known as normal distribution statistical tests. The statistical methods of inference make certain assumptions about the populations from which the samples are drawn. For example, the assumptions may be that the populations are normally distributed, have the same variance, etc.; population values, as we have seen, are known as parameters; the statistical techniques which make assumptions about the parameters are called parametric techniques

Nonparametric tests: Researchers in the field of health sciences many times may not be aware about the nature of the distribution or other required population parameters. In addition, sample may be too small to test the hypotheses and generalize the findings for the population from which the sample is drawn. Furthermore, many times in the observations presented in numerical figures, the scale of measurements may not be really numerical, such as grading bedsores, or ranks given to analgesic drug's effectiveness in cancer pain management. In these situations, parametric tests may not be suitable, and a researcher may need different types of tests to draw inferences; those tests are known as nonparametric tests.

Q 14. Analysis of Variance (ANOVA) Test

$$=$$

When a researcher wants to compare the difference between more than two samples means; t-test I will be useful and a need of alternative test will be felt. This need can be fulfilled by test known as analysis of variance (ANOVA) test.

Therefore, it is clear that ANOVA is used to compare the more than two sample means drawn from corresponding normal population. For example, a researcher wants to examine the difference in effect of ginger on three difference conditions such as nausea, vomiting, and retching, here t-test can be applied to examine difference in the mean scores, because there are more than two groups; therefore, ANOVA will be used in this case.

Steps of application of ANOVA

Calculate the total of submission of all the group of observations. Calculate the sum squares of all the observations.

Calculate the total of sum of squares by using following formula;

$$= \Sigma X^2 - \frac{(\Sigma X)^2}{N}$$

- Calculate the sum of squares between the groups by using following formula.

$$= \frac{(\Sigma \bar{X}_1)^2}{n_1} + \frac{(\Sigma \bar{X}_2)^2}{n_1} + \frac{(\Sigma \bar{X}_3)^2}{n_3} + \frac{(\Sigma \bar{X}_4)^2}{n_4} + \cdots \text{so on} - \frac{(\Sigma \bar{X})^2}{N}$$

- Calculate the sum of squares within the groups (error sum of squares) by using following formula:
  = Total sum of squares – sum of squares between the groups

- Calculate the degree of freedom for between and within the groups.

  df for between the groups = number of groups – 1
  df for within the groups = number of subjects in all the groups – number of groups
  df total is = number of subjects in all the groups – 1.

- Calculate the mean of sum of squares by using following formula:

$$\text{Mean of sum of squares between the groups} = \frac{\text{Sum of squares between the groups}}{\text{df for between the groups}}$$

$$\text{Mean of sum of squares within the groups} = \frac{\text{Sum of squares within the groups}}{\text{df for within the groups}}$$

Finally compute the F-ratio by using following formula:

F-ratio of square =

Mean of sum of squares between the groups

Mean of sum of squares within the groups

the tabulated 'F" value for horizontal (df of between the groups) and vertical df (of within the groups) at the specified level of significance such as .05, 01, etc. If calculated 'F' value is more than tabulated 'F' value, then we reject the null hypothesis. If calculated 'F" value is less than tabulated 'F' value, then we accept the null hypothesis.

’F‘ value is less than tabulated ’F' value, then we accept the null hypothesis.

Q15. *Vancourvers style of reference.*

= Vancouver style. Vancouver is a numbered referencing style commonly used in medicine and science, and consists of: Citations to someone else’s work in the text, indicated by the use of a number.

Vancouver is a numbered referencing style commonly used in medicine and science, and consists of:

- citations to someone else's work in the text, indicated by the use of a number
- a sequentially numbered reference list at the end of the document providing full details of the corresponding in-text reference

It follows rules established by the International committee of Medical Journal Editors, now maintained by the U.S. National Library of Medicine. It is also known as Uniform Requirements for Manuscripts submitted to Biomedical Journals.

Before using this guide check with your faculty, school or department for their specific referencing guidelines

In-text citations

- Insert an in-text citation:
    - when your work has been influenced by someone else's work, for example:
        - when you directly quote someone else's work
        - when you paraphrase someone else's work

- General rules of in-text citation:
    - A number is allocated to a source in the order in which it is cited in the text. If the source is referred to again, the same number is used.
    - Use Arabic numerals (1,2,3,4,5,6,7,8,9)
    - Either square [ ] or curved brackets ( ) can be used as long as it is consistent. Please check with your faculty/lecturer to see if they have a preference. For consistency in this guide we have chosen to use round brackets for our examples
    - Superscripts can also be used rather than brackets eg. ...was discovered. [1,3]
    - Reference numbers should be inserted to the left or inside of colons and semi-colons.
    - Reference numbers are generally placed outside or after full stops and commas - however check with your faculty/journal publisher to determine their preference. For consistency in this guide we are placing reference numbers after full stops.
    - Whatever format is chosen, it is important that the punctuation is consistently applied to the whole document.

Multiple works by the same author:

Each individual work by the same author, even if it is published in the same year, has its own reference number.

Citing secondary sources:

A secondary source, or indirect citation, occurs when the ideas on one author are published in another author's work, and you have not accessed or read the original piece of work. Cite the author of the work you have read and also include this source in your reference list.

The in-text citation is placed immediately after the text which refers to the source being cited:

Using round brackets:

...as one author has put it "the darkest days were still ahead".(1)

Using square brackets:

...as one author has put it "the darkest days were still ahead".[1]

Using superscript:

...as one author has put it "the darkest days were still ahead".[1]

The author's name can also be integrated into the text

Scholtz[1] has argued that...

Including page numbers with in-text citations:

Page numbers are not usually included with the citation number. However should you wish to specify the page number of the source the page/s should be included in the following format:

...as one author has put it "the darkest days were still ahead".[1(p23)]

...as one author has put it "the darkest days were still ahead".(1 p23)

Scholtz (1 p16-18) has argued that...

Citing more than one reference at a time:

The preferred method is to list each reference number separated by a comma, or by a dash for a sequence of consecutive numbers. There should be no spaces between commas or dashes

For example: (1,5,6-8)

Reference List

- References are listed in numerical order, and in the same order in which they are cited in text. The reference list appears at the end of the paper.
- Begin your reference list on a new page and title it 'References.'
- The reference list should include all and only those references you have cited in the text. (However, do not include unpublished items such as correspondence).
- Use Arabic numerals (1, 2, 3, 4, 5, 6, 7, 8, 9).
- Abbreviate journal titles in the style used in the NLM Catalog
- Check the reference details against the actual source - you are indicating that you have read a source when you cite it.

Writer Information

Name : Rutwik Upendra Bhalshankar.
Mobile NO : 9130024431
Mail: rutwik61@gmail.com